A LETTER

FROM GOVERNOR POWNALL
TO ADAM SMITH

A
LETTER
FROM
GOVERNOR POWNALL
TO
ADAM SMITH, L.L.D., F.R.S.

BEING AN

EXAMINATION OF SEVERAL POINTS OF DOCTRINE

LAID DOWN IN HIS

INQUIRY INTO THE NATURE AND CAUSES
OF THE WEALTH OF NATIONS

[1776]

THE ADAM SMITH LIBRARY

REPRINTS OF ECONOMIC CLASSICS

AUGUSTUS M. KELLEY · PUBLISHERS
NEW YORK · 1967

FIRST EDITION 1776
(London: J. Almon, *Opposite Burlington-House,
in Piccadilly*, 1776)

Reprinted 1967 by
Augustus M. Kelley Publishers

Library of Congress Catalogue Card Number

« 66 - 15563 »

PRINTED IN THE UNITED STATES OF AMERICA
by SENTRY PRESS, NEW YORK, N. Y. 10019

A

LETTER

FROM

GOVERNOR POWNALL

TO

ADAM SMITH, L.L.D. F.R.S.

A

LETTER

FROM

GOVERNOR POWNALL

TO

ADAM SMITH, L.L.D. F.R.S.

BEING AN

EXAMINATION OF SEVERAL POINTS OF DOCTRINE,

LAID DOWN IN HIS

"INQUIRY INTO THE NATURE AND CAUSES OF

THE WEALTH OF NATIONS."

LONDON:

Printed for J. ALMON, oppofite Burlington-houfe, in Piccadilly.

M DCC LXXVI.

The Reader is defired to correct the following Errata, which efcaped notice in correcting the Prefs. Copy from the Manufcript.

P. 13, l. 3, for *more*, read *mere*.
P. 27, l. 26, for *think*, r. *thing*.
———————————*tend*, r. *tends*.
P. 28, l. 24, for *at firft that*, r. *that at firft*.
P. 34, l. 1, in the note, for *motion*, r. *money*.
P. 45, l. 25, for *great knowledge*, r. *information*.

There are alfo one or two errors in the pointing, which were not attended to, but which the Reader will be fo good to rectify.

A

L E T T E R, &c.

SIR,

WHEN I firſt ſaw the plan and ſuperſtructure of your very ingenious and very learned Treatiſe on the Wealth of Nations, it gave me a compleat idea of that ſyſtem, which I had long wiſhed to ſee the publick in poſſeſſion of. A ſyſtem, that might fix ſome firſt principles in the moſt important of ſciences, the knowledge of the human community, and its operations. That might become *principia* to the knowledge of politick operations; as Mathematicks are to Mechanicks, Aſtronomy, and the other Sciences.

Early in my life I had begun an analyſis, of *thoſe laws of motion* (if I may ſo expreſs myſelf) which are the ſource of, and give direction to, the labour of man in the individual; which form that reciprocation of wants and intercommunion of mutual ſupply that becomes *the creating cauſe of community*; which give energy, motion, and *that organized form* to the compound labour and operations of that community, *which is government*; which give ſource to trade and commerce, and are the forming cauſes of the inſtrument of it, *money*; of the effect of it in operation, an *influx of riches*, and of the final effect, *wealth and power*. The fate of that life called me off from ſtudy. I have however at times (never totally loſing ſight of it) endeavoured to reſume this inveſtigation; but fearing that the want of exerciſe and habit in thoſe intellectual exertions may have rendered me unequal to the attempt, I am extremely happy to find this executed by abilities ſuperior to what I can pretend to, and to a point beyond that which the utmoſt range of my ſhot could have attained. Not having any perſonal knowledge of the author, or of the port which I now underſtand he bears in the learned world, I read your book without prejudice.—I ſaw it deſerved a more cloſe and attentive application, than the ſeaſon of buſineſs would allow me to give to it; I have ſince in the retreat of ſummer ſtudied it: you have, I find, by a truly philoſophic and patient analyſis, endeavoured to inveſtigate *analitically* thoſe principles, by which nature firſt moves and then conducts the operations of man in the individual, and in community: And then, next, by application of theſe principles to fact, experience, and the inſtitutions of men, you have endeavoured to deduce *ſynthetically,*

tically, by the moſt preciſe and meaſured ſteps of demonſtration, thoſe important doctrines of practice, which your very ſcientifick and learned book offers to
the conſideration of the world of buſineſs.

Viewing your book in this light, yet ſeeing, as my reaſoning leads me to
conceive, ſome deviations which have miſled your analyſis, ſome aberrations
from the exact line of demonſtration in the deductive part; and conſidering
any errors in a work of that authority, which the learning and knowledge
that abounds in yours muſt always give, as the moſt dangerous, and the
more ſo, as they tend to mix themſelves in with the reaſoning and conduct of
men, not of ſpeculation, but of buſineſs—I have taken the liberty, by ſtating
my doubts to you in this Letter, to recommend a reviſion of thoſe parts which
I think exceptionable.

If theſe doubts ſhould appear to you to contain any matter of real objection, I ſhould hope thoſe parts might be corrected, or that the bad conſequences of thoſe poſitions, which I conceive to be dangerous, may be obvia-
ted. When I firſt wrote theſe obſervations, I meant to have ſent them to
you, by the interpoſition of a common friend, in a private letter; but, as I
think theſe ſubjects deſerve a fair, full, and publick diſcuſſion, and as there
are now in the world of buſineſs many very ingenious men, who have turned
their minds to theſe ſpeculations, the making this publick may perhaps ex-
cite their ingenuity, and thus become the means of eliciting truth in the moſt
important of all ſciences. It may animate even your ſpirit of inquiry, and
lead to further reſearches. It is not in the ſpirit of controverſy, which I both
deteſt and deſpiſe, but in that of fair diſcuſſion that I addreſs this to you.

When, in your inveſtigation of thoſe ſprings, which give motion, direction,
and diviſion to labour *—you ſtate " *a propenſity to barter;*" as the cauſe of
this diviſion : when you † ſay, " that it is that trucking buſineſs which *originally*
" gives occaſion to the diviſion of labour;" I think you have ſtopped ſhort in
your analyſis before you have arrived at the firſt natural cauſe and principle of
the diviſion of labour. You do indeed ‡ doubt, " whether this propenſity
" be one of thoſe *original principles* in human nature, of which no farther ac-
" count can be given; or whether, as ſeems more probable, it be the neceſ-
" ſary conſequence of the faculties of reaſon and ſpeech." Before a man can
have the propenſity to barter, he muſt have acquired ſomewhat, which he does
not want himſelf, and muſt feel, that there is ſomething which he does want,
that another perſon has in his way acquired; a man has not a propenſity to
acquire, eſpecially by labour, either the thing which he does not want, or
more than he wants, even of neceſſaries; and yet nature ſo works in him,
he is ſo made, that his labour, in the ordinary courſe of it, furniſhes him in
the line in which he labours, with more than he wants; but while his labour
is confined in that particular line, he is deprived of the opportunity to ſupply
himſelf

* B. I. C. II.   † P. 18.   ‡ P. 16.

himfelf with fome other articles equally neceffary to him, as that which he is in the act of acquiring. As it is with one man, fo is it with the next, with every individual, and with all. Nature has fo formed us, as that the labour of each muft take one fpecial direction, in preference to, and to the exclufion of fome other equally neceffary line of labour, by which direction of his labour, he will be but partially and imperfectly fupplied. Yet while each take a different line of labour, the channels of all are abundantly fupplied.

Man's wants and defires require to be fupplied through many channels; his labour will more than fupply him in fome one or more; but through the limitation and the defined direction of his capacities he cannot actuate them all. This limitation, however, of his capacities, and the extent of his wants, neceffarily creates to each man an accumulation of fome articles of fupply, and a defect of others, and is the original principle of his nature, which creates, by a reciprocation of wants, the neceffity of an intercommunion of mutual fupplies; this is the forming caufe, not only of the divifion of labour, but the efficient caufe of that community, which is the bafis and origin of civil government; for, by neceffarily creating an inequality of accumulation, and a confequential fubordination of claffes and orders of men, it puts the community under that form, and that organization of powers, which is government. It is this principle, which, operating by a reciprocation of wants in nature, as well as in man, becomes alfo the fource to that intercommunion of fupplies, which barter, trade, and general commerce, in the progrefs of fociety, give. It is not in the voluntary defires, much lefs in a capricious " *propenfity to barter*," that this firft principle of community refides; it is not a confequence of reafon and fpeech actuating this propenfity, it is interwoven with the effence of our nature, and is there in the progrefs of, and as part of that nature, the creating and efficient caufe of government; of government as *the true ftate of nature* to man, not as an artificial fuccedaneum to an imagined theoretic ftate of nature.

The purfuing of the Analyfis up to this *firft principle*, does not immediately, I agree with you, " belong to the fubject of your inquiries;" for the doctrine contained in the fecond chapter of your firft book, feems only noted *en paffant*, but is no where, either in the courfe of your Analyfis, ufed, nor applied in the fubfequent explications. But as fome thirty years ago, I had made this Analyfis of the * *Principles of Polity*; and as I have, in the practical adminiftration of the powers of government, found, that thofe powers on one hand do, as from the trueft fource, derive from thefe principles of nature, and

---

* A little Treatife which I wrote when I was very young, and which is very imperfect and incorrect in its manner and compofition; but fuch in the matter and reafoning, as frequent revifion and application of the principles to matters in fact, have confirmed me in the conviction of as true, although different from the common train of reafoning in thofe who follow Mr. Locke's phrafes rather than his arguments.

that

that the liberties of mankind are moſt ſafely eſtabliſhed on them: and as I think that great danger may ariſe to both, in deriving the ſource of community and government from paſſions or caprice, creating by will an artificial ſuccedaneum to nature, I could not but in the ſame manner, *en paſſant*, make this curſory remark.

Having eſtabliſhed and defined this firſt operation of man in community, that of *barter*, you proceed to conſider the *natural rules* by which this is conducted; what it is which gives *value*; what it is which *meaſures* the relative or *comparative value*, and hence the doctrine of *price*: and by the intervention of theſe, *the introduction of money and coin*. As in the former doctrine, I thought you had not purſued the analyſis to the real ſources of nature; ſo here, on the contrary, I think you have ſtretched your doctrine beyond the garb of nature. Some of your more refined doctrines have rather ſubtiliſed ideas, as they lie in your mind, than analiſed thoſe diſtinctions which lie in nature. On the firſt reading the eight firſt chapters of your firſt book, in which theſe matters are treated of, before I came to the uſe and application of your doctrines in the explication of practice and buſineſs, I began to apprehend, that ſome dangerous conſequences in practice might be deduced from theory, inſtead of thoſe ſound and beneficial doctrines which derive through experience, by a true analyſis of nature and her principles. I thought I ſaw, that many miſchievous impertinent meddlings might take riſe from a diſtinction between *a natural* and *a market price*. As I had been uſed to hold that only to be the meaſure of exchangeable value, which the world generally takes and uſes as ſuch, money formed of the precious metals; I could not but apprehend, that many extenſively dangerous practices might ariſe from your laying aſide, in your Analyſis of Money, the idea of its being A DEPOSIT. I ſaw, that that *theory in metaphyſicks*, led to a deſtructive *practice in phyſicks*; to the practice of creating a *circulation of paper*, and of calling ſuch circulation, money; and of introducing it as ſuch. In your doctrine, that " labour is the meaſure of " exchangeable value of all commodities," connected with your mode of explanation of the wages of labour, the profit of ſtock, the rent of land, and the effect of the progreſs of improvements, I thought I ſaw great danger, that Theory, in the pride of rectitude, might harden its heart againſt the real, though relative, diſtreſſes, which the labourer and the landed gentry of a country do ſuffer, and are oppreſſed by, *during the progreſs* of improvement, in conſequence of a *continuing influx of riches*; and might therefore depreciate, or even endeavour to obſtruct, all thoſe current remedies which give comfort and relief to theſe diſtreſſes, and alleviate even thoſe which cannot be remedied.

Although * the demand for thoſe who live by wages muſt naturally increaſe with the increaſe of national wealth; and conſequently the price of wages riſe in proportion to the riſe of every thing elſe; ſo as that the labourer will in the

end

* Pag. 85.

end partake of the general riches and happiness of the publick. Although * the rise in the price of all produce is in the end no calamity, but the *forerunner* of every publick advantage : Yet as those prices do *forerun*, and muft, during the progrefs of improvement, *always forerun*; wages and rent muft always continue *at an under-value* in the comparifon. They will indeed rife alfo, but as this foreruns, they can only follow, *fed non paffibus æquis.* The labourer, and he who lives on rent, therefore, muft always, though improving, be un-able to improve fo faft as to emerge from a continued diftrefs : if this diftinc-tion, that a flowing encreafe of wealth, although it is the forerunner of every advantage to the publick in general, and *in the end* to every individual, yet is the continuing caufe to the continued diftrefs of the labourer, and of him who lives by rent, is not carefully attended to. If the ftate of the circumftances of diftrefs, which continues to opprefs thofe claffes of the community, are not conftantly adverted to with feeling, and with exertions of precaution and be-nevolence, we fhall, in the triumph of our general profperity, be the conftant oppreffors of thofe who have the beft title to fhare in this profperity.

Under thefe ideas and apprehenfions I did very carefully and repeatedly, be-fore I proceeded to the applied doctrines contained in the latter book, revife the analytic part of the former. When I came to the doctrines applied to practice, and the bufineffes of the world, I found that my cautions had not been unneceffary, and that my apprehenfions, that fome fuch confequences might be drawn from it, were grounded : I found alfo what I did not from the principles expect (nor as yet do I fee how they derive from them, as any part of the chain of reafoning) that in the courfe of the doctrines you hold, you are led to difapprove the law giving a bounty on corn exported; and alfo to think, that the monopoly, which we claim in the American trade *, " like all other mean and malignant expedients of the mercantile fyftem," without in the leaft increafing, doth on the contrary diminifh the induftry of the country, in whofe favour it is eftablifhed; and doth, although it may have the feducing afpect of a *relative advantage* †, fubject the nation, its trade and commerce, to an abfolute difadvantage. I hope you will not think, that I mifunderftand, or mean to mif-ftate, your pofition. You allow, and very fully explain the great advantages of the colony trade, but think that the monopoly is the reafon why, great as it is, we do not derive fo great advantages from it to the nation and to the landed intereft, and to the community in general, as we might have done, had it not been crampt and perverted by the monopoly.

In the many occafions which I have had to view this monopoly, I own, al-though I have feen fome errors in the extenfion of the *meafure*, further than is expedient or neceffary, yet I do not fee the malignancy of the principle of a monopoly; nor while I have lived amidft the daily proofs of the *relative ad-vantage* which it gives to the mother country, by its colonies, over all other

foreign

---

* Pag. 286. † B. IV. C. VII. P. 201.

foreign nations, I have not been able to difcover, nor have your arguments, although fo methodically and fo clearly drawn out, been able to explain to me, that abfolute difadvantage which you think it fubjects us to.

Although I agree entirely with you, having alfo previoufly read the fame opinion in Mr. Necker's Treatife, *fur la Legiflation & le Commerce des Graines*, that the bounty which our law gives to the exportation of corn, has not been the fole caufe which hath rendered corn cheaper than otherwife it would have been; but, on the contrary, hath, in each direct inftance, given it fome fmall advance in the general fcale of prices: Yet, confidering that fo far as it does this, and gives relief to the relative oppreffion which the landed intereft muft continue to feel under *a continued influx of riches*, and an advancing rife in the prices of every thing elfe; I think it one of the wifeft meafures for a country like England that could be devifed.

I think with you, that many of our laws and regulations of trade are practical errors, and mifchievous. I think that, while they feem to be founded on our navigation act, they miftake the fpirit of it, and no lefs miftake the real intereft of the nation: yet I cannot but hold thefe to be errors only, as they deviate from the true principle of the act of navigation, which is a different thing from the acts of trade.

Having prefaced thus much as to the feveral doctrines on which I have conceived fome doubts, I will now, following the order of your work, ftate thofe doubts. When I found you difcarding *metallic money*, that intervening commodity which having, by common confent, acquired a value of its own, hath been hitherto efteemed a common known meafure of the value of all other things, from being any longer fuch common meafure, and by a refinement of theory, endeavouring to eftablifh in its place " an abftract notion," *that labour was the common meafure of all value*; I did not only doubt the truth of the pofition, but, looking to the ufes that might be made of the doctrine, hefitated on the principle. If labour be the only real and ultimate meafure of value, money is but the inftrument, like the counters on the checquer, which keeps the account; if this be all the ufe of money, then *circulation*, or even *an account opened with a banker* (according to a practice in Scotland, as defcribed by you) is to all ufes and ends as good as money. If it is not neceffary, that the common meafure fhould have fome known permanent value in itfelf, fo as to be a depofit of that abfent value which it reprefents, as well as meafures, fo as to convey to all who poffefs it an abfolute power of purchafe, then indeed the circulating inftrument, the machine that circulates, whether it be a paper or a leather one, or even an account, without any *depofit*, is equal to all the ufes and end of money, is that which we may fafely receive for the future. As I have been mixed in the bufinefs of a country, where the evils of this doctrine and practice have been feverely felt, and where it was my duty to watch, that nothing was impofed upon the publick as money, but what was either in itfelf

felf a depofit, or was eftablifhed on a fund equal to a depofit, and what had *a'l* the ufes of a permanent known meafure in all cafes of circulation ; I could not but read this leading doctrine of your's with great caution and doubt. I muft doubt, whether it be labour fimply which creates and becomes the meafure of value, when I find other component parts mixed in the moft fimple idea of value : I cannot conceive, that equal quantities of labour are abfolutely of equal value, when I find the value of labour both in ufe and in exchange varying in all proportions, amidft the correlative values of thefe components parts ; I cannot fuppofe labour to be the ultimate meafure, when I find labour itfelf meafured by fomething more remote.—You fay very properly in the major of your fyllogifm, that when the divifion of labour has once thoroughly taken place, it is but a very fmall part of the neceffaries and conveniencies of life, with which a man's own labour can fupply him. But when we come to the minor propofition of it, we muft confider alfo the objects on which labour is employed; for it is not fimply the *labour*, but the *labour mixed with thefe objects*, that is exchanged ; it is *the compofite article, the laboured article :* Some part of the exchangeable value is derived from the object itfelf; and in this compofite value, which is the thing actually exchanged, the labour bears very different proportions of value, according to the different nature of the object on which it is employed. Labour, employed in *collecting* the *fpontaneous produce* of the earth, is very different in the compofite exchangeable value of the fruit collected, from that which is employed in raifing and collecting the *cultured fruits* of the earth. Labour, employed on a rich, cleared, fubdued and fruitful, or on a poor and unkindly foil, or on a wild uncleared wafte, has a very different value in the compofite object produced in the one, from what it bears in the compofite value of the other. As the object then makes part of the compofite value, we muft confider, in the exchangeable value, the object alfo, as a component part. Whofe then is the object ? Who has acquired, and does poffefs, the object or objects on which the labour may be employed ? Let us take up this confideration under thefe firft fcenes of man, which are ufually called a ftate of nature, fomewhat advanced in the divifion of labour and community. Previous to the employing of labour, there muft be fome acquifition of objects whereon to employ this labour ; a ftrong and felfifh man, who will not labour, fits, we will fuppofe, idly under a tree, loaded with the fpontaneous fruits of nature ; an induftrious, but weaker man, wants fome part of thofe to fupply his neceffity, the idler will not let him collect the fruit, unlefs that other collects alfo enough for both. Or if, ftill more churlifh and more felfifh, he will not let him who is willing, by his labour, to collect a fufficiency for *his* ufe, unlefs the labourer collects alfo more than fufficient for the idler's prefent ufe, fufficient for his future ufe alfo. Does the labourer here command or exchange, by his labour, any part of the labour of the idler? Certainly not. In this ftate *a divifion of*
the

the objects on which labour muft be employed, and with which it muft be mixed, as well as a divifion of labour hath taken place; and therefore the labourer muft be able, by his labour, to command in exchange a certain portion of thefe objects which another hath, as well as a certain part of that other's labour. It will not relieve this doubt by faying, as Mr. Locke (treating of right) fays, that there can be no *right of poffeffion*, but by a man's mixing his labour with any object; becaufe we are here not confidering the matter of right, but the matter of fact: nor will it anfwer to fay, that the acquifition itfelf is an act of labour, becaufe I have here ftated the cafe of a churlifh fluggard idler, ftrong enough to maintain himfelf in idlenefs, by commanding not only the actual labourer, but certain *greater or leffer quantity of that labour*, according as his felfifh churlifh temper leads him to prefs upon the neceffity of the weaker. Suppofe the fame idler, in this divifion of the objects of labour, to have got poffeffion of a fifhing lake, or a beaver-pond, or in a fandy defart of a fpring; or of a fpot of fruitful ground, amidft a barren country; or of a ford, or particular pofition, which commands a fine hunting-ground, fo as to exclude the labourer from the objects whereon his labour muft be employed, in order to form that laboured article which is to fupply his wants. You fee, that the means of commanding the *objects of labour, as well the labour* of another, make part of the fupply whereby a man muft live, whereby he may be faid to be rich or poor. Even you yourfelf (I hope you will excufe the expreffion under which I quote it) fay, with rather fome degree of confufion in terms, " that every thing is really *worth* to the man who has acquired it, and who " wants to difpofe of it, or exchange it for fomething elfe; the toil and trouble " which it can fave to himfelf, and which it can impofe upon other people." This expreffes the conclufion which I draw from the cafe I have ftated, and not your pofition, that labour is the *meafure*, and that it is labour which is exchangeable for *value:* it is, on the contrary, the mixture of the labour, and the objects laboured upon, which produces the compofite value. The labour muft remain unproductive, unlefs it hath fome object whereon to exert itfelf, and the object is of no ufe unlefs laboured upon. The exchange therefore is made by A keeping a part of his labour mixed with a part of the object, and B ufing a part of his objects rendered ufeful by the labour of A mixed with them. The confequence therefore in your fyllogifm cannot fairly conclude, that the value of any commodity to the perfon who poffeffes it, and who means not to ufe or to confume it himfelf, but to exchange it for other commodities, *is equal to the quantity of labour*, which it enables him to purchafe or command. On the contrary, it is a compofite value of the object and labour mixed, and takes part of its value from each of the component parts. It is not therefore labour (which is but one of the component parts of the exchangeable commodity) which gives the exchangeable value, but *the labour and the object mixed*, the compounded laboured article, in which the labour bears all

poffible

poſſible proportions to the correlative value of the two component parts, according as the poſſeſſor of the object, or the exertor of the labour, or the common general courſe of the eſtimation of mankind ſhall ſettle it. Real value, if any ſuch thing there be different from market value, is *the mixed compoſite laboured article*, not labour ſimply.

You have, Sir, made a very proper diſtinction of *value in uſe*, and *value in exchange*. That labour which varies in its productive power, according as it is differently applied, and according to the object it is employed upon, muſt certainly vary in its uſe, and equal quantities of it muſt be in ſuch different circumſtances of very unequal value to the labourer. *Labour in vain, loſt labour—Labour which makes itſelf work*, (phraſes which, to a proverb, expreſs ſome ſpecies of labour,) *cannot be* ſaid to be *of any uſe* to the labourer. He who would ſhave a block with razor, will labour in vain. He who ſows on a rock, or on a barren ſand, or in a drowned moraſs, will loſe his labour. He who ſheers his hogs, will have great cry and little wool, and only make himſelf work : but labour will ſtill vary more in its *exchangeable value* ; equal quantities of labour will receive very variable degrees of eſtimation and value. In the firſt operation of barter of labour (the value of the objects being, for the ſake of argument, laid aſide) we will ſuppoſe A to ſay to B, you ſhall have as much of the ſurplus of my labour on the article ○, as you will exchange for the ſurplus of your labour on the article △. By this, A " means to ſave " as much of his toil and trouble to himſelf, and to impoſe as much upon B, " as he can." B means the ſame. What then is to be the real ſtandard of meaſure ? Not labour itſelf. What is to give the reſpective eſtimation in which each holds his labour ? Each alternately will be diſpoſed to eſtimate his own moſt valuable, and to each " the labour of the other will ſometimes appear to " be of greater and ſometimes of ſmaller value *." This value cannot be fixed by and in the nature of the labour ; it will depend upon the nature of the feelings and the activity of the perſons eſtimating it. A and B having, by equal quantities of labour, produced equal quantities of two of the moſt neceſſary articles of ſupply, whoſe values, in the general ſcale of things, vary the leaſt ; each having a ſurplus in the article which his labour has produced, and each likewiſe having an equal want of what the other has produced. This *quantity* of labour, although ſtated as *equal*, will have very different *exchangeable values* in the hands of the one or the other, as A or B are *by nature* formed to make a good bargain in the common adjuſtment of the barter. He who has not an impatience in his deſire on one hand, or a ſoon-alarmed fear on the other of loſing his market ; who has a certain firmneſs, perſeverance and coldneſs in barter ; who has a certain *natural* ſelf-eſtimation, will take the lead in ſetting the price upon the meek and poor in ſpirit ; upon the impatient and timid bargainer. The higher or lower value of theſe equal quantities of labour,

* Pag. 39.

labour, will follow the one or the other fpirit. The value is not equal, and is not fixed in, nor depends upon, the equal quantity of the labour; it is unequal and differs, and is fixed by, and derives from, the different *natures of the perfons* bargaining. The exchangeable value of equal quantities of labour, ftated equal in all circumftances, is not only not equal in this firft inftance, between that of A and B, but may, in other comparifons, vary both in A and in B individually. The exchangeable value of B, although inferior in barter with A, may acquire an afcendant value, and be fuperior in barter with C. This difference and this variation will run through every degree in the utmoft extent of the markets: nay, the fame perfon will, in different habits, relations and circumftances of life, eftimate that labour (which fhall be ftated to be abfolutely equal) as of very different value; he will, on different occafions, eftimate his " eafe, liberty, and defire of happinefs" differently. Equal quantities of labour, equal, I mean abfolutely, and in every refpect, will acquire and derive very different values both in ufe, and in exchange both in refpect of the perfon by whom fuch is exerted, as well as in refpect of the perfon who barters for it, from the objects with which it is mixed. Refpecting the perfon by whom it is exerted, if a day's labour always produces a day's fubfiftance, the value in ufe is always the fame; if it doth not, the value in ufe muft vary. In refpect of exchangeable value, labour will fometimes give value to things which, in themfelves, had little or no value: in others, it will derive value from the things with which it is mixed; it will itfelf have an exchangeable value from its compounded value; that is, from the proportion of value which it bears in the compofite laboured article.

What is thus varying in a relative value, muft require fome correlative, which, while this meafures other things, in return will meafure it; that which is itfelf meafured by fomething more remote, cannot be the final meafure or ftandard. It cannot * therefore be " alone the ultimate and real ftandard by " which the value of all commodities can, at all times and places, be efti- " mated and compared: it is not their *real price*." I muft therefore conclude, in a propofition which I quote from yourfelf, where I wifh you had let the bufinefs † reft; " That there can be no accurate meafure, but that exchange- " able value muft be fettled by the higgling and bargaining of the market, ac- " cording to that fort of rough equality, which, though not exact, is fuffici- " ent for the carrying on the bufinefs of life."

You confefs, that this propofition of your's, " *That labour is the meafure* " *of the value, and the real price of all commodities*," is " *an abftract notion*." As fuch I fhould not have taken any notice of it; but you endeavour to eftablifh it as a leading principle, whereby I think a *practical one*, which mankind hath univerfally and generally acted upon, may be in dangerous fpeculations diftinguifhed away. If the common forenfick idea, that money which,

in

* Pag. 39. † Pag. 37.

in the common acceptation of it, hath actually been ufed to meafure, doth in ftrict truth meafure as " a common intervening commodity," both labour and all other things, and their relations, is to be confidered as a more practical notion, and we are in reafoning to look to fome abftract notion, as the real ftandard. What do we, but pervert our reafoning from diftinct notions in practice, to " abftract notions," and fubleties in theory : as I apprehend that thefe theories have been, and fear they may and will again be ufed, if admitted into the reafoning of the world, to very mifchievous and deftructive fchemes ; as I think that they remove old bounds, and erafe old and folid foundations, and may be applied to the building paper caftles in the air ; as they lead to fpeculations, which fwerve from the idea of *pledge and depofit in money matters*, and tend to create *an imaginary phantom of circulation*, erected on the foundation of credit and opinion of truft only, I have taken the liberty of ftating my doubts upon it.

While I have thus doubted, whether labour is the ultimate meafure and ftandard of the exchangeable value of all commodities, I fhould be willing with you to admit, that corn will not univerfally anfwer as fuch a meafure, had not you yourfelf*, in another part of your book feemed to think, that " the " nature of things has ftamped upon corn, *a real* value, which no human in- " ftitution can alter ; and that *corn* is that regulating commodity, by which " the real value of all other commodities muft *be finally meafured* and deter- mined." Gold and filver, you fay, varying as it doth in its own value, can never be an accurate meafure of the value of other things. There is then, ac- cording to what I have always been ufed to think, and what from your Trea- tife I find myfelf confirmed in, no one commodity that will meafure all others, but that all are to one another in their reciprocal value *alternate meafures* ; and that *gold and filver* is only the common and moft general, almoft the univerfal, meafure, fo found to be, and fo ufed by the general experience and confent of mankind, as *that intervening commodity* which will moft uniformly become *a common meafure*, at the fame that it doth (as being a depofit of value, which all mankind have agreed to receive) *give univerfal power of purchafe.*

As I think that there is no real meafure of value, fo I think there is no fix- ed natural rate of value, or real price diftinct from the market price. I think, that the doctrine which ftates the two definitions as an actual exifting truth, and as a practical diftinction formed for bufinefs, not true on one hand, but on the other a dangerous propofition.

You fay, † " That there is in every fociety or neighbourhood *an ordinary or* " *average rate* both of wages and profit, in every different employment of la- " bour and ftock ;" thefe average rates you call " the *natural price,* at the " time and place in which they commonly prevail."

The

* B. IV. C. V. Vol. II. P. 101.   † B. I. C. VII. P. 66.

The actual price at which any commodity is *commonly fold,* is called its market prince.

I clearly fee the diftinction in definition; but I do not learn how the ordinary average rates, or price paid for labour, or for the ufe of land or ftock, or for any commodity in the neighbourhood, where it comes from the firft hand, in the firft act of bargain and fale, is any more natural than the price which it finds and bears in any other fucceeding act of bargain and fale, at the time and place wherever it is fold. What is it, in the firft inftance, which fettles thefe average rates, which you call natural, but the competition of the effectual demand, compared with the fupply, and founded on fome proportion whereby the price paid for labour, ftock or land, will enable the feller to purchafe an equivalent quantity of thofe neceffaries and conveniences which his ftate of life requires? If, from this firft operation of bargain and fale, the commodity, by means of carriage, and the collection, ftorage, and diftribution of the middle man, goes to a fucceeding and more complicated value with thefe adventitious articles of expence added to it : Is not the price which is here, alfo the price at which it here commonly fells, and which is in like manner precifely determined equally, that ordinary average rate and *natural price* as the former? Or rather, is not the price in the firft operation of bargain and fale *equally a market price* as the latter, fettled by that higgling and barter which doth and muft finally regulate it in all times and in all cafes? The refinement which, ufing different expreffions, as in one cafe calling it " the ordinary average rate," and in the other, " that price at which it is com- " monly fold," is a diftinction of words without fcarce a difference in idea, certainly none in fact and truth. If there be any fuch thing as a natural price, both are natural; if not, which I rather think both are the artificial market price, fuch as the act of higgling and barter can fettle on the reciprocation of wants and mutual fupply. What elfe is it in *nature* which fettles the ordinary average rates, which you call the natural price? This price " *naturally* " increafes," as adventitious circumftances mix with the commodity brought to fale. The encreafed market price encreafes by the adventitious circumftances of labour in carriage, of rifque, ftorage, and the middle-man's profit. This encreafe is *naturally* regulated by the ordinary and average rates of thefe added circumftances in their time and place; and on thefe the competition, compared with the fupply, doth as naturally in one cafe as in the other create the market price; which may be called, if you choofe to call the former fo, a natural price; but both are, in fact, equally in their time and place the market price. When therefore you fay, * " that the natural price is the *central* " *price,* to which the prices of all commodities are perpetually gravitating;" I muft own that I receive the metaphor of the propofition with great apprehenfions of the ufes in practice, which the doctrine may lead to. If any one, who

* B. I. C. VII. P. 70.

who has got a lead in bufinefs, fhould adopt your diftinction of *natural and market price*; and, following the delufion of your metaphor, fhould think, that, as in nature, all market prices do perpetually gravitate to the natural *central price*, fo the circuiting motion of all market prices fhould be made to take and keep this direction round their center; (perfectly fatisfying himfelf, that as he ought not, fo he does not, meddle with the *natural prices* of things:) he may, through a confufion and reverfe of all order, fo perplex the fupply of the community, as totally to ruin thofe who are concerned in it, and intirely to obftruct it. He may render trade almoft impracticable, and annihilate commerce. That the fucceeding prices of the fecondary operations of bargain and fale are regulated by the fame rules and laws of barter as the firft; and that the outfet of the firft will give direction of motion, as well as motion to all fucceeding operations, regulated by the fame laws of this motion, is certainly true; and that it will (while in the ordinary courfe of things) keep this motion equable by the refpective average rates in their time and place: that the violence and artifices of man will ever and anon try to warp and mifrate it, is certainly true; and a truth well worthy of conftant attention—not with a view to interfere and intermeddle with the *market prices*, under any theory of regulating them by fome fuppofed natural *central price*, but to obftruct and oppofe all interference and meddling whatfoever; and upon this truth to maintain in the market an univerfal freedom, choice and liberty.

Although, as I have ftated my opinion above, I think, that the general courfe of all prices, or that correlative value between commodities muft depend upon, and derive from the reciprocal higgling of bargain and fale, and are not meafured by labour: Yet fo far as they depend upon, or are mixed with labour, there is fome natural fcale below which they cannot go; which fcale takes its level from the quantity of fubfiftence which fuch labour will procure. The plain and home-fpun wifdom of our anceftors, therefore, did not attempt to meafure the prices of things by any *abstract notion of labour being that meafure*, but they meafured labour itfelf * " by the plenty or dearth of provifions," or the fubfiftance, according to the laboured productive effects of nature from time to time. Although therefore I agree with you, † " that the *common wages* of " labour *depends* every where *upon the contract* made between two parties, " whofe interefts are by no means the fame;" yet in that, ‡ " a man muft " always live by his work, and that his wages muft at leaft maintain him." There is a fcale of rate below which the price of labour cannot by any contract or bargain be lowered.

That the prices of wages do continually increafe with the advancing profperity of any community, and that they are the higheft in thofe communities, who are advancing with the moft rapid velocity, is a truth, a comfortable and an encouraging truth: yet as prices of wages follow but with flow and loaded

E fteps,

* Vide the feveral ftatutes of labourers. † B. I. C. VIII. P. 81. ‡ P. 83.

steps, in proportion to the quick motions of the rise of the prices of all other things, if some care and attention is not given to aid the motion of the rise of wages, in some measure to keep it above the lowest scale, which it can subsist by; we may, in the triumph of prosperity, and in the pride of rectitude, see the poor labourer, of the lower classes, under a continued state of helpless oppression, amidst the prosperity of the community in general; but of the nature, and of the manner of regulating these, I shall have occasion to treat in another place, and on another occasion.

As value or price is not any fixed *natural* thing, but is merely the *actual* correlative proportion of exchange amongst all commodities; *so that intervening commodity which* does in fact most commonly, or on common result, and by common consent, *express this correlative proportion*, is *the common measure* of this value: It is not an abstract notion of *labour*, " but *money* * (as " Mr. Hume says) which is *by agreement* the common measure." This common measure does not barely express the proportion of value between commodities when brought together in the act of exchange, but is that something, that most common intervening commodity, which mankind hath generally and universally agreed shall not only express this act of exchange, and the relation of reciprocal value under which it is made, but which is in fact an universal equivalent deposit of value, which gives, in all places and at all times, with all persons, a power of purchase, and is in fact and truth that intervening commodity, which, as a common measure, exchanges without actually bringing the things exchanged into barter. The thing which we thus express in abstract reasoning by the word *money*, is *by use* universal, by general and common consent, *the precious metals applied as this practical common measure*, the uses which it hath, and the purposes to which it is applied amongst the acts and things of the community, gives it *a value in its exchangeable operations*. This idea of money is fixed by *old bounds* of common consent and universal practice; and as I am not willing *to remove old bounds*, fixed in a real foundation, to follow an abstract notion † " on Dædalian wings through the air;" I will here next take the liberty to state the reasons which make me hesitate to follow you in those regions of theory. Although you tell me, that it is not the metallic money which is exchanged, it is the *money's worth*; that money may be the *actual* measure of this exchange, but that it is the labour which the money represents and sells and purchases, which is the *real measure*. Yet when my ideas lead me in the very line of your analysis to conceive, that labour is not, no more than any other commodity, the ultimate measure, but is the thing measured; that when measured against subsistence, it is actually measured by that subsistence. When I consider, that although it is the money's worth which is exchanged, yet it is the money which measures and exchanges it. I cannot but think it nearest even to abstract truth, and safest in practice,

to

* Essay on Money, P. 321.　　　† B. II. C. II. P. 289.

to abide by *the old bounds* of that idea which mankind hath generally and univerſally fixed, *that money* IS THE COMMON MEASURE, to be which adequately, and in all its *uſes*, it muſt be a DEPOSIT alſo.

In your account * of the origin and uſe of money, you very properly ſtate, that " every prudent man in every period of ſociety (after the firſt eſtabliſh-
" ment of the diviſion of labour) muſt naturally have endeavoured to manage
" his affairs in ſuch manner, as to have at all times by him, beſides the pecu-
" liar produce of his own induſtry, a certain quantity of ſome one commo-
" dity or other, ſuch as he imagined few people would be likely to refuſe in
" exchange for the produce of their induſtry." If in the doing this, all, led by any thing in the nature of any commodity itſelf, or by ſome coincidence of reaſoning and conſent, ſhould agree upon any one commodity in general, which would be thus generally and univerſally received in exchange, *that*, in the moſt refined ſtrictneſs of abſtract reaſoning, as well as in deciſive fact, would become that † *intervening commodity* which would meaſure the exchangeable value, and be the real inſtrument of actual exchange in the market. It would not only be that *meaſure*, but it would become a *real* as well as *actual deposit of value*, and would convey to whomſoever poſſeſſed it, a general, univerſal and effective power of purchaſe.

When next then I inquire, what this intervening commodity is—I find, ‡ that metallic money, or rather " ſilver, is that which, by the general con-
" ſent of mankind, has become that depoſit, which is the common meaſure;
" this is a general effect of ſome general cauſe. The experience of its degree
" of ſcarceneſs, compared with its common introduction amidſt men, toge-
" ther with the facility of its being known by its viſible and palpable proper-
" ties, hath given this effect. Its degree of ſcarceneſs hath given it a value
" proportioned to the making it A DEPOSIT; and the certain quantity in
" which this is mixed with the poſſeſſions and tranſactions of men, together
" with the facility of its being known, has made it A COMMON MEASURE
" amongſt thoſe things. There are perhaps other things which might be bet-
" ter applied to commerce as *a common meaſure,* and there are perhaps other
" things which might better anſwer *as a deposit*; but there is nothing, except
" [the precious metals, or rather] ſilver, known and acknowledged by the
" general experience of mankind, which is *a deposit and a common meaſure.*
" Paper, leather, or parchment, may, by the ſanction of government, be-
" come a common meaſure, to an extent beyond what ſilver could reach; yet
" all the ſanction and power of government never will make it an *adequate* de-
" poſit. Diamonds, pearls, or other jewels, may, in many caſes, be conſi-
" dered as a more apt and ſuitable depoſit, and may be applied as ſuch to an
" extant to which ſilver will not reach: yet their ſcarcity tends to throw them
" into

* B. I. C. IV. P. 28. † C. V. P. 37. ‡ Vide adminiſtration of the Colonies, C. V. Vol. I.

" into a monopoly; they cannot be fubdivided nor amaffed into one concrete;
" and the knowledge of them is more calculated for a myftery, or trade, than
" for the forenfic ufes of man in common, and they will never therefore be-
" come a common meafure.

" The quantity of this depofit, and the general application of it to feveral
" different commodities, in different places and circumftances, creates a cor-
" relative proportion between it and other objects, with which it ftands com-
" pared, and from this proportion forms *its own fcale*; this fcale derives from
" the effect of natural operations, and not from artificial impofition. If there-
" fore filver was never ufed but by the merchant, as the general meafure of
" his commerce and exchange, *coin* would be (as it is in fuch cafe) of no ufe;
" it would be confidered as bullion only. Although bullion is thus fufficient
" for the meafure of general commerce, yet for the daily ufes of the market
" fomething more is wanted in detail; fomething is wanted to mark to com-
" mon judgment its proportion, and to give the fcale: government therefore
" here interpofes, and by forming it into COIN gives the fcale, and makes it
" become to forenfic ufe AN INSTRUMENT in detail, as well as it is in bullion
" A MEASURE in general."

It is here, Sir, that I think your Analyfis, fubtilifed by too high refinement, deviates from the path in which the nature of things would have led you.
Quitting the idea of money being A COMMON MEASURE, and totally leaving
out all idea of its being a DEPOSIT, your Analyfis leads you to conceive no
other idea of it but as CIRCULATION, or, as you diftinctly exprefs it, a CIRCU-
LATING MACHINE; and of courfe, according to thefe principles, confidering it as an inftrument, you ftate it in your account *amongft thofe inftruments
which form the fixed capital of the community.* The refult of which in fair
reafoning is, that as thefe machines coft an expence (which muft be either
drawn from the circulating capital of the community, or from its revenue by
favings) both to erect them and to maintain them; fo every faving which
can be made in the erection or maintenance of fuch a machine, will be advantageous to the circulating capital, the fource of materials and wages, and
the fpring of induftry. In this line of deduction you come to the refult in
practice, and fay, * that " the fubftitution of paper, in the room of gold
" and filver money, replaces *a very expenfive inftrument* of commerce with one
" much lefs coftly, and *fometimes* equally convenient; *circulation* comes to be
" carried on by *a new wheel,* which it cofts lefs both to erect and to maintain
" than *the old one.*"

As my reafoning hath many years ago impreffed it ftrongly on my mind that
money is a COMMON MEASURE, and muft be a DEPOSIT, and *in coin an inftrument* of the market; and as many years experience in a country of paper
hath convinced me, that if any inftrument of the exchange of commodities,

other

---

* B. II. C. II. P. 350.

other than that which, while it meafures the correlative values in circulation, is founded on a DEPOSIT, equivalent at all times to the converfion of it into money, fhall be introduced, it will be a fource of fraud, which, leading by an unnatural influx of riches to luxury without bounds, and to enterprize without foundation, will derange all induftry, and inftead of fubftantial wealth end by bankruptcies in diftrefs and poverty.

So far as *circulation* can carry on the exchanges of commodities in the community, fo far paper bills of credit, or even accounts opened, may do in the room of the metallic money; but without a depofit, which is adequate and equivalent in all times and places, and with all perfons, to this converfion of it, I have no fure foundation, that I do poffefs, in all times and places, and with all perfons, *the power of purchafing or of accumulating as I like.* Although I have all the truft and confidence in the world in the credit of this circulating machine of paper, yet it has not the univerfal extent in, nor the operation of all the ufes of money, although therefore it may be " *fometimes* " *equally convenient;*" it is not that intervening commodity which hath *all the ufes of money,* * univerfally and adequately. Circulation, even where no paper money or credit exifts, muft always much exceed in its total of exchange the fum total of the money depofit, how much that is, experience in the fact can alone determine : paper may certainly, without any danger, encreafe this power of circulation, if it does not exceed what the depofit will anfwer while it is in circulation, and is created *on fuch a fund, as will finally convert it into money.* So far as paper, by the extent of the ufes, and the abfolute fecurity and exchangeable converfion of it into metallic money, *can be and is made a depofit,* fo far it may fafely meafure as money, and become a convenient inftrument; but in that this fecurity is always more or lefs uncertain; in that it depends on the prudence and probity of the money-makers, it is always liable to exception, abufe and failure. So far forth as it is defective in its fund, the creation and ufe of it muft be always hazardous, and hath been generally ruinous; and however diftant and remote the end may be, *muft* be a fraud in the end. In a world of enterprize,, where *truft and credit* is fubftituted *in the ftead of fund* and prompt change, paper money lofes the very effence of a depofit; unlefs I have *a depofit,* which gives me an abfolute actual power of purchafing, in all times and places, in all events, to all intents and ufes; or that which is abfolutely ready and immediate change for fuch depofit. The bill which I have, may or may not, here or there, now and then, *fometimes* not always, maintain in me *the power of purchafing,* or of real hoarding or banking as I like. General, univerfal, permanent confent of all mankind, has from *actual experience* of its ufes, given to *metallic money* a permanent and abfolute value : partial, local, temporary agreement, founded *in opinion of truft and credit,* can give to paper but a partial, local, temporary ideal value, which never

will

* P. 350.

will be a real and univerfal depofit; it may become to certain local temporary purpofes a *circulating machine*, but money is fomething more : this paper is not that intervening commodity, which all mankind hath univerfally agreed to be *that common meafure which is a depofit*; fuch alone is money in the ftrict as well as common acceptation of the word and idea.

So far as paper money can be fo contrived as to have, while it is in circulation, *a l the ufes* of money; or is fo founded, that it can in all moments and in all places be taken out of circulation by converfion into metallic money at its nominal value, fo far it will be equal to money both as a meafure and as a depofit. But fo far as it is defective in any one ufe, however much it may ex-cel in any other ufe, it will and muft depreciate below the real value of the metallic money, which it is fuppofed to reprefent; fo far as in any point of time or place the power of converting it into metallic money is remote, fo far is it ideal, unfubftantial, and no depofit. Although with a fund of 20,000*l.* a banker, or the treafury of a government, may circulate 100,000*l.* yet as whenever, for any reafon, or by any event, it becomes neceffary to take that 100,000*l.* out of circulation, the banker or the treafury can but pay 20,000*l.* or four fhillings in the pound, that circulation muft end in a fraud.

Where, in the circulation of capital, paper money is fubftituted inftead of metallic money, you allow, that it will not anfwer in its ufes to foreign trade. I, for the fame reafon, add, it will not *pay taxes*, fo far as thofe taxes are to *fupply expences incurred or laid out abroad*. If great variety of *reabforbing glands* did not in Scotland take up, in the courfe of circulation, the amount of the taxes levied on that part of the kingdom, their paper money could not pay that amount.

Juft as much gold, as paper circulation becomes a fubftitute for, may be fpared from circulation, and will become, as you truly fay, a new fund for commerce, and will go abroad in foreign trade : if it is employed in a commerce of luxury or confumption, it is in every refpect hurtful to fociety; fo far as it purchafes raw and rude materials, or provifions or tools, and inftruments to work with, it may be beneficial. You think that, however individuals may run into the former, bodies and focieties are more likely to actuate the latter. Yet in countries where a fuperabundant quantity of paper money hath taken place, where the power of creating this money hath advanced fafter in its creation and emiffions than the labour, induftry and abilities of the inhabitants would have produced it. This *artificial plenty* hath always encouraged a commerce of luxury; an over-trading; a multitude and difproportionate number of fhop-keepers; extravagant expences in idle land-holders; more building than can be fupported; and all kinds of ambitious and dangerous projects. " * The commerce and indufty of a country, you muft ac-" knowledge, and do candidly confefs, though they may be fomewhat augment-" ed, cannot be altogether *fo fecure,* when they are thus, as it were, fufpend-

" ed

* B. II. C. II. P. 389.

" ed upon the *dædalian wings of paper money,* as when they travel *on the solid*
" *ground of gold and silver.* Over and above the accidents to which they are
" expofed from the unfkilfulnefs (*I would here add the fraud alfo*) of the con-
" ductors of this paper money, they are liable to feveral others, from which
" no prudence or fkill of the conductors can guard them."—You indeed rea--
fon from the *abufe,* but all thefe arguments do equally derive from the *defect* of
this paper money. As it creates an *influx of riches,* which does not fpring from
induftry, which is not the effect and produce of ufeful labour; it creates, with
aggravated circumftances, all that diftrefs which the real ufeful labourer and
real man of property, the land-owner, muft feel, even under an influx of real
riches; it gives motion and velocity to this influx, without producing any real
depofit whereon the *riches,* which it pours in to circulation, *may be funded as*
WEALTH. The land-holder lives for a while under oppreffion and diftrefs;
he then, raifing his rents beyond what the real ftock will bear, lives in a de-
lufive abundance of luxurious expence, but is finally ruined. The fucceffor,
who purchafes him out, fucceeds by the fame difeafe to the fame ruin. The
labourer, and all who live on fixed ftipend, are under a continued feries of oppreffion. The falfe wealth only of adventurers, jobbers, and cheats, become
the riches of the country; that real depofit, which would be a fund of real
wealth and real fupply in cafe of diftrefs, will be chaced away. The phantom
of circulation, which is fubftituted in its place, will, inftead of coming in
aid, fail, and vanifh on the firft alarm of diftrefs.

" * An unfuccefsful war, for example, in which the enemy got poffeffion
" of the capital (*who does not tremble as he reads ?*) and confequently of that
" treafure which fupported the credit of paper money, would occafion *a much*
" *greater confufion* in a country where the whole circulation was carried on by
" paper, than in one where the greater part of it was carried on by gold and
" filver. The ufual inftrument of commerce *having loft its value,* no ex-
" changes could be made but by barter or upon credit. All taxes having been
" ufually paid in paper money, the prince would not have wherewithal either
" to pay his troops or to furnifh his magazines; and the ftate of the country
" would be much more irretrievable, than if the greater part of its circula-
" tion had confifted in gold and filver. A prince, anxious to maintain his
" dominions in a ftate in which he can moft eafily defend them, ought, upon
" this account (*and I add upon all others*) to guard not only againft the excef-
" five multiplication of paper money, which ruins the very banks that iffue
" it, but even againft that multiplication of it, which enables them to fill the
" greater part of the circulation with it."

I was willing to oppofe, in your own words, this fair defcription which you
give of the dangerous ftate of a country which abounds in *circulation of riches,*
inftead of a depofit, which is *wealth,* as an antidote againft the delufions of

this

* B. II. C. II. P. 389.

this powerful temptation: and as I think the dose ought to be repeated, I will repeat it in the words of the very clear-minded and ingenious Mr. Hume *.

" He has entertained *(he says from similar reasons as above stated)* a great " doubt concerning the benefit of banks and paper credit, which are so gene- " rally esteemed advantageous to every nation. That provisions and labour " should become dear, by the encrease of trade and money, is, in many re- " spects, an inconvenience, but an inconvenience that is unavoidable, and the " effect of that publick wealth and prosperity, which is the end of all our " wishes. It is compensated, however, by the advantages which we reap, " from the possession of those *precious metals,* and the weight which they give " the nation in all foreign wars and negotiations. But there appears no rea- " son for the encreasing that inconvenience by *a counterfeit money,* which fo- " reigners will not accept in any payment, and which *any great disorder in the* " *state will reduce to* NOTHING."

It is for these reasons, because I am not for *removing old bounds,* and that I wish to preserve the old general established opinion, that money is a *common measure;* because I am unwilling to receive that *new and delusive friend* CIRCULATION, instead of *the old and steady one,* MONEY, which being a DEPOSIT, will stick by us in all times, that I have taken the liberty to examine this part of your Analysis, and to wish, if you should be persuaded to revise it, that you would enquire, in the real track of nature, whether that commodity, by the inter- vention of which the exchanges of all commodities may in all times and cases be actuated, must not, *in truth as well as fact,* be that common measure, in the use of which all mankind have universally agreed, and must not be a deposit, which the metallic money alone is: and whether, where paper circu- lation is not so proportioned to the deposit as that, that deposit is always ready to exchange it during its circulation; is not established on such a *fund* as will *absolutely exchange it;* whether, I say, such paper circulation is not a delu- sion that must finally, however remotely, lead to a fraud.

By what I have said above I do not mean to say, that paper is not useful; I think, that under such due regulations respecting the FUND, which is to ex- change it, the USES to which it is to be applied, and the QUANTITY in which it may be safely issued, as will make it a common measure and a DEPOSIT, it is not only generally beneficial, but that the greatest advantages may be derived from it to the publick.

If now, Sir, by these principles, as I have stated them, as they are found in the FUND and the USES, you examine all the schemes of paper circulation from that of the bank of Amsterdam, founded on a real deposit, to that of the Scotch banks, founded on † trust and confidence, without any actual deposit; if you examine the paper money, and the operations of that wise and prudent institu- tion, the loan-office of Pensylvania, examine the foundation and the succeed-
ing

* Hume's third Essay on Money. † B. II. C. II. Vol. I. P. 351.

ing operations of the bank of England, you will find, that you have a fixed canon, by which you may precisely mark what are real, what delusive; what may be beneficial, what will be ruinous in the end. Whereas, if no other idea but that of *circulation* enters into our notion of money; if it be conceived to be nothing more than *a circulating machine,* under that conception every delusive fraudulent credit, which every adventurer can establish *on a deceived and betrayed confidence,* may set in motion a circulation, that may on every ground be justified even in the moment of its bankruptcy. And even those just and wise precautions, with which you have endeavoured to guard this circulation against fraud, may tend to give an opinion of confidence to this circulation, when it shall be so guarded, which in any case it ought not to have, unless it can be so framed as to have *all the use* of money in circulation, and be so *funded* as in the end to be a real deposit.

It is impossible to pass over those parts of your learned work, wherein you treat of labour, stock, and land; of wages, profit, and rent; of the monied prices of commodities, and especially your very curious and scientifick Treatise on the Precious Metals applied as Money; it is impossible to read those parts respecting the effects of the progress of improvement in the community, of the nature, accumulation, and employment of stock, without reiterating the idea and the wish expressed in the beginning of this letter, of seeing your book considered as INSTITUTE OF THE PRINCIPIA *of those laws of motion,* by which the operations of the community are directed and regulated, and by which they should be examined. In that part, however, which explains the different effect of different employment of capital, wherein you seem rather to have engrafted some foreign shoots, than to have trained up, in the regular branchings of your Analysis, to propositions fully demonstrated, I will beg to arrest your steps for a moment, while we examine the ground whereon we tread; and the more so, as I find these propositions used in the second part of your work as data; whence you endeavour to prove, that the monopoly of the colony trade is a disadvantageous commercial institution.

After having very justly described the four different ways in which capital stock may be employed—first, in drawing from the elements of earth and water the rude, the spontaneous or cultured produce; next, in working these materials up for use; next, the general exchange or trade of these commodities, conveyed from place to place as they are wanted; and, lastly the retail distribution of them to the consumer. After having divided by fair analysis the general trade or commerce, described under the third head, into three different operations—that is, the home trade; the foreign trade of consumption, and the carrying trade. After having shewn the just gradation of beneficial employ of capital, which these different operations produce, and how truly beneficial each in its respective *natural* gradations is, * " When the course of
" things,

* B. II. C. V. P. 453.

" things, without any conftraint or violence, naturally introduces it ;" you lay and prepare a ground of contraft, from whence in your fourth book to prove, that the eftablifhment of a monopoly in the colony trade, by perverting this *natural order and gradation of operations* in commerce, hath rendered the commerce of fuch colonies lefs beneficial than they might otherwife in general have been ; I am here marking only the order of your argument, not trying the force of it. In the order of this argument, I think I difcover an effential mifconception of that branch and operation of commerce, which is in nature *circuitous*, and as fuch beneficial ; but which you conceive to be and call *a round-about commerce*, and as fuch of courfe, and in the nature of things, difadvantageous. Your argument goes to prove, that the monopoly, inftead of leaving the direct trade to its full and free operation, inftead of fuffering the round-about trade (as you call it) to take up the *furplus only* of capital which that produces, and next the carrying trade naturally to abforb what the others difgorge, doth force capital, which might have been more beneficially employed in a direct trade, into a round-about trade ; which is too commonly miftaken for the carrying trade of Great Britain.

I mean, in its place, to examine this your argument, in your application of it to the actual fubject. I will here, in the mean time, with your leave, make an affay of the truth of its combination ; for it appears to me, that in treating *a circuitous commerce* as a *round-about trade*, you confound two things the moft diftinct in their nature, and the moft different in their effect of any two that could have been put together.

A CIRCUITOUS TRADE or commerce is that by which receiving, *with the due profits of return of capital*, fome article of trade or fome commodity, *which is better to go to market with than money*, I go to market with that commodity fo received ; and perhaps again with fome other in like manner received ; and perhaps again with a third, making by each operation my due profits, annexed to each return of my capital ; and finally a greater fuperlucration of profit than I could have done by the fame number of direct trades ; and confequently either a greater revenue, or a greater accumulation of capital, that may again employ more productive labour.

A ROUND-ABOUT TRADE, on the contrary, with loft labour, with wafte of expence, and unprofitable detention of capital, fends to market fome commodity (as the proverb well expreffes it) *by Tom-Long the carrier.*

We will fuppofe, that the Britifh merchant or factor hath fold his Britifh manufactures in Virginia, in which he vefted his capital ; and that he has it in fpeculation, whether by taking money, a bill of exchange, or fome commodity, which is ready money's worth in the Britifh market, he fhall make a direct return of his capital, and its fimple accretion of profit ; or whether by taking fuch commodities, as by an intermediate operation in his way home, he

may

may derive an intermediate adventitious profit from, before the fame is again reinvefted in Britifh goods for the Virginian market.

In the firft cafe, his capital may be faid to return with its profit directly; in the fecond, although it may make a circuit, and be detained awhile in its way home, yet it is not detained, nor goes out of its way *unprofitably* to Great Britain; for by the fuperlucration, arifing from the intermediate operation, it gives proportionably either a greater revenue, or as an encreafed capital employs more productive labour.

We will fuppofe a fecond cafe taken up on this fpeculation, that he either receives corn by barter, or by purchafe invefts what he has received in that commodity, with which, inftead of coming directly home, he calls in his way at Cadiz or Lifbon; the fale of his corn there returns him his capital with a fecond accretion of profit. Here again he fpeculates in like manner, and determines to inveft this accumulated capital in wines, fruits, &c. which at the home market will again return his capital, with farther accretion of profit. Has not every movement of this circuitous trade been a different operation? Has not each operation made a diftinct return of capital? Has not each return given its peculiar profit? Has any expence been wafted? Any labour loft? Has there been any detention of capital unprofitably to Great Britain, while, at its return, it affords either more revenue, or, as capital, employs more productive labour than otherwife it would.

Let us in another line fuppofe, that this merchant or factor receives tobacco, rice, indigo, or peltry, which he brings directly home; with thefe commodities at the Britifh market he fpeculates, whether he fhall take ready money there for them, which, vefting in Britifh mannfactures, or foreign manufactures bought with Britifh produce, he will return directly to Virginia again with. Or whether thefe commodities, which reprefent his capital, with its accretion of profit, might not ftill more encreafe it, if he himfelf fent them to that market where they are purchafed for confumption. We will fuppofe, that his prudence directs him to the latter conduct. He fends them then to Ruffia or to Germany. They there return him his capital, with another accretion of profit. We will fuppofe, that he re-invefts his capital with hemp or flax for the Britifh, or in linnens for the American market. He is by this operation enabled to go back again to America, either with Ruffian or German manufactures, bought with Britifh commodities, or felling what he bought of Ruffia or Germany in the Britifh markets, with a ftill more increafed quantity of Britifh manufactures than what any direct trade between America and Great Britain could have purchafed. Here again the fame queftions may be afked, and muft receive the fame anfwers.

On the contrary, wherever there is a *round-about trade*, there the commercial operations are obftructed, and the advantages greatly defalcated, if not,

in

in many inftances, entirely loft. The obliging the merchant to bring rice from the fouthern latitudes northward to Great Britain, which rice muft go back again fouth to its market in the fouthern parts of Europe and the Streights, was a round-about trade, it was labour loft, it was a wafte of expence, an unprofitable detention of capital, and the commodity was fent by *Tom Long the carrier* to market. The monopoly therefore, in that cafe, where it created a round-about trade, hath been relaxed. Sugars are in the fame cafe; and a like relaxation, under peculiar regulations relating to that peculiar article, have been recommended, and might be fafely and beneficially given. There are fome parts of the tobacco crops, which, in the affortment, might be admitted to fomewhat a fimilar liberty without danger, but with benefit. Nay, *that intermediate operation of the circuitous trade,* mentioned above, which obliges the Virginian tobacco to come to England before it goes to Germany, and the German linnens alfo to come to England before they go to America, *is a round-about trade,* a needlefs and very difadvantageous operation, in which fome relaxation ought to be made. I can fee, that the Englifh merchant may lofe a commiffion, but labour and expence would be faved to the community. In like manner the obliging the Weft India fhips, which, fince the interruption of the American trade, load ftaves, lumber and corn in England, which articles are brought from foreign parts, is obliging them to take up thefe things by a round-about trade; whereas, if they were permitted to fhip, in Britifh fhipping only, thefe articles at the foreign markets directly for the Weft Indies, many inconveniencies, which the Britifh part of the community experiences, might be avoided, and both labour and expence faved to the community at large. If falt fifh, which is intended for the fouthern markets, was obliged to be brought northward firft to England, and fo go round about to the fouth, its proper market, it would create a round-about trade. If thefe fhips loading with falt for their back carriage were obliged to come round by England, it would create a round-about trade, and in either cafe would wafte labour, and might lofe all the profit of the capital employed. The monopoly therefore does not take place in this.

The permitting, in certain cafes ftated, and under certain regulations fpecified, the Americans who go with fifh directly to the Streight, Spain, or Portugal, to purchafe there, if purchafed of Britifh merchants, certain articles, and to carry the fame, fo purchafed, directly back to America, fo far as it would avoid the round-about trade, perfevering, and even extending at the fame time the Britifh market, has been for twelve or fourteen years fucceffively recommended.

I think in general on this fubject, that wherever the monopoly would create a round-about trade, it fhould not take place; and that wherever it hath occafioned any fuch round-about operation, it fhould be relaxed; always

ways however keeping in view this object and end, namely, that so far as our colonies are to be confidered as an inftitution, eftablifhed and directed to encreafe the naval force of our marine empire, and fo far as that force derives in any degree from the operations of their commercial powers, fo far that monopoly, which engrafts them upon our internal eftablifhment, is indifpenfible, and ought never to be departed from or relaxed. The fovereign power, which hath the care of the defence and ftrength of the empire, ought never to permit any the moft flattering idea of commercial opulence to come in competition with the folid ground of ftrength and defence. In this way of reafoning I find myfelf joined by you, who reafon in the fame way, and almoft in the fame words, when fpeaking of the act of navigation you fay, that, " although it be not favourable to foreign commerce, or to the growth " of that general opulence which might arife from it, yet, as defence " is of much more importance than opulence, it is the wifeft of all the " commercial regulations of England". On the ground and deriving my reafoning from the fame principle, I fay, that the monoply is of the fame fpirit; is not only wife, but is alfo neceffary, and that it is not the monopoly, but the injudicious undiftinguifhing application of it, without that reafon which alone can juftify it, and in channels where it neceffarily creates a round-about trade, which renders it difadvantageous, not only to the colonies, but to the general community of the empire.

As no round-about trade, unlefs where the obliging the colony trade to fubmit to fuch, is neceffary to the fyftem of defence, fhould be occafioned, but fhould even, where it has taken place, be relaxed, fo, on the contrary, * I have always thought, that a circuitous operation in the colony trade, as the think which of all others tend moft to increafe and extend the American markets for Britifh manufactures, fhould be allowed and encouraged, provided that trade in its circuition keeps its courfe *in an orbit that hath Great Britain for its center.*

Having thus fhewn, fimply to the point of ftating the cafe, not arguing it, that a circuitous commerce and a round-about trade are two very different and diftinct things, having very different operations and very different effects: having fhewn that the circuitous trade is very advantageous, while a round-about trade is always detrimental, but that the circuitous commerce of the colonies is not that hurtful round-about trade which you treat as occafioned by the monopoly, I will now proceed to examine, under their feveral heads, your application of the principles which you lay down in your analyfis, as what directs your fynthetic reafonings on the commercial inftitutions which have taken place in the Britifh œconomy.

* Vide Adminift. of the Britifh colonies, Vol. I. C. VIII.

Although

Although I perfectly agree with you, that the *restraints on the importation* of such foreign goods as can be produced cheaper at home are useless; and that the laying restraints on the importation of such as cannot be made so cheap at home, answers no good end, but may be hurtful; although I allow, that these measures, as a kind of institution of monopoly in favour of internal industry in preference, or to the exclusion of the produce of foreign industry coming to it, does not always tend to encourage the home industry, but, on the contrary, gives a false turn to it, puts it on a false ground and profit, and may have the effect of forcing an unprofitable labour: yet I am unwilling to quit the principle of encouraging the first efforts of home industry, if employed on home commodities in the home market, as I think the principle, applied only in cases where it is wanted, may be very beneficial; I had rather, in my notions of political œconomy, abide by the principle, and examine, upon each application of it, how it does or does not operate to encourage a profitable industry, skill and habit in peculiar branches of labour, which the society has to learn, and which learnt will be profitable. If a society, which once used to send abroad its rude produce to purchase manufactures made of that very rude produce so sent out, and which it knew not how to work up, had never been, by some adventitious aid, over and above what the sources of the first efforts of its industry could have given, encouraged to begin in trials of its skill; if the individual is not, while he is learning his trade, and the skill of working profitably in it, supported in part, he can never attempt to learn it; if the society does not pay for the learning, it can never have it; although it be true at first that the *apprentice* (for by that name I will express the first efforts of a manufacture) is not employed to the greatest advantage, because he might buy the articles which he is learning to make, cheaper than he can make them; although the community pays this difference; although these efforts, thus artificially forced, are at first disadvantageous and unprofitable to the community: yet by his industry being so directed to, and so supported in a line of labour, which he could not naturally have gone into, nor could have supported himself by, these first efforts, which the community pays for, do by repeated exercise produce skill, which in time will work as well, and enable the home manufacturer (if his labour is *employed on native home rude produce*) to sell as cheap, and soon cheaper, than the foreign workman and manufacturer; his labour then will become profitable to himself, and advantageous to the community of which he is a part. It was thus our woollen and hardware manufactures were first encouraged and supported; but the very same principle, and the same reasoning upon it, hath always led me to a persuasion, that no aids of a monopoly in the home market, nor no bounties, can ever force a manufacture founded and *employed on foreign rude materials*. It is an attempt, by robbing Peter to pay Paul, to establish a trade,

the

the natural profit of which cannot support the eſtabliſhment, and the loſs of which muſt be made up to it by payments from the ſociety at large. Againſt ſuch your principle, in the full force of its arguments, ſtands unanſwerable. Such is the linnen manufacture wrought on foreign line and flax; ſuch is the ſilk in ſome degree; this laſt, however, ſo far differs, as that rude material may be imported full as cheap as any rival country in Europe can raiſe it.

You think, the reſtraints upon the importation of live cattle and corn an unreaſonable and ungenerous monopoly, for that the grazing and farming buſineſs of Great Britain could be but little affected by a free importation of theſe, and not in the leaſt hurt. As, on the contrary, I think, any change in this part of our ſyſtem might be attended with the moſt important conſequences, eſpecially to a claſs of people who bear the chief burthen of all the taxes, and are the ſupport of the ſtate of the community. I own, I tremble for the change, and ſhould hope this matter may be a little more thoroughly explored, in all the effects of its operation, before any ſuch idea becomes a leading doctrine.

You have with clear and profound reaſoning * ſhewn, that in an improving ſtate of the community, the prices of cattle and of butchers meat, and the leſſer articles of the ſupply muſt ſtart, and continue to riſe until they come to ſuch a rate, as ſhall make it worth the farmer's while to cultivate the land, which he rents, to the purpoſes of breeding and feeding ſuch cattle, and to the raiſing theſe other articles for the market; this you properly call *the natural progreſs of improvement*, and theſe riſing values *the natural courſe of prices*. If a free importation of cattle and of theſe leſſer articles ſhould be allowed, this *adventitious ſupply* coming from countries which have great waſtes for breeding cattle, which do not pay ſuch heavy taxes, and which are not arrived at that degree of improvement in which this country is found, ſuch importation *muſt derange this ſcale of natural prices, and muſt arreſt this progreſs of improvement in its courſe.* If ſuch foreign country can breed and feed, and afford to import and bring to market cattle and theſe leſſer articles cheaper than our grazer can, the grazing buſineſs at home muſt ceaſe. Well—but ſay you, if under theſe circumſtances grazing will not anſwer, the land will be broken up for tillage. But here again, if a free importation of corn, on a like plan, derived from ſuch reaſoning on theſe principles, is, as you recommend, permitted, that branch of buſineſs, not capable of farther extenſion, and met at market by ſuch importation, will be at a ſtand, and finally become retrogade; we ſhall be obliged to give up all our improvements, and return to our waſtes and commons. In order to obviate in ſome meaſure theſe objections, a kind of diſtinction is made between the importation of lean and fat cattle.

The

* B. I. C. II. Part III.

The importation of lean cattle would not, fays the argument, hurt, but be-nefit the feeding farms. The breeding farms, however, would be ruined; and there is a link of connection, which fo allies the whole progrefs of country bu-finefs in one chain of intercommunion, that all in the end would fuffer and be undone.

A fecond palliative ufed to obviate thefe objections, which naturally arife againft this idea of giving up our fyftem of reftraints on importation of cattle, * is, that the importation of *falt provifions* could never come in competition with the frefh provifions of the country. To try how this would operate, let us fuppofe that the Victualling-Office, as the law now ftands, is in the ordinary courfe of taking great quantities of cattle, and in the extraordinary demand which war occafions, takes off a proportionate encreafed number; this of courfe raifes the price of the grazers fales, and countervails, in fome meafure, with the landed intereft, the burthen of the encreafed taxes. But if a free im-portation of falt provifions is to take place as a fettled fyftem, the Englifh gra-zer, while the war encreafes his burthens, and raifes the price of every article which he purchafes, is himfelf met at the market by a competition brought againft him from a country that does not bear this encreafed burthen; and he cannot therefore find that *natural fcale of price*, which the maintenance of his bufinefs and relative ftate in the country requires; he muft be ruined, and the land foon rendered incapable of paying its rents, and of raifing thofe very taxes.

In the fame train of reafoning you think, that a free importation of corn could very little affect the intereft of the farmers of Great Britain, becaufe the quantity imported, even in times of the greateft fcarcity, bears fo incon-fiderable a proportion to the whole ftock raifed. From this argument, found-ed in fact, you think the farmers could have nothing to fear from the freeft importation; and you reproach them on the account of the fyftem of reftraint againft free importation of corn, as forgetting the generofity which is natural to their ftation, in demanding the exclufive privilege of fupplying their coun-trymen. If here, Sir, you had weighed well a diftinction which Monf. Necker † has, with exquifite precifion, explained, you would have fpared this reproach. It is not the ratio of the quantity of corn exported or imported, and the quantity of the whole ftock raifed, but the ratio between the *furplus* and this quantity exported or imported, which creates the effect; it is not a ratio of $\frac{1}{577}$, but a ratio of $\frac{1}{15}$, which acts and which operates on the market; it is not the $\frac{1}{577}$ part, but the $\frac{1}{15}$th part which would operate to the depreffion of the market and the oppreffion of the farmer.

Chearful under the burthen of the taxes, and fpiritedly willing to pay them in fupport of his country, he only wifhes to enable himfelf to do fo from his induftry, and the natural profits of it at his own market, without having that

market

* Vol. II. P. 41.   † Sur la Legiflation & le Commerce des Graines.

market loaded from an external fupply, and depreffed by a competition from countries which are not in that ftate of improvement, and do not pay thofe taxes, which he muft add to his price, if he is to live and pay them; he does not defire the *exclufive* fupply, but a fair and equal market on the natural fcale of prices, which fhall give vent to his fupply; this furely he may do without reproach. On the contrary, were it poffible to fuppofe that the country gentleman could be perfuaded to change the fyftem, and give up the fecurity which the reftraint on importation gives him in his intereft, he would defervedly incur the real reproach of having loft that practical fenfe, which the country gentlemen have always hitherto been found to have, when they come to real bufinefs.

But I think you rather mifreprefent our fyftem of reftraint on importation of corn; it does not abfolutely prohibit corn from being brought into the country, and does not eftablifh *an exclufive fupply* in the country land-owner; it only reftrains fuch an importation as may either in quantity or price injure the free and fair vent of our own fupply in our own market, at fuch prices as the general ftate of the improvement of the community and the fcale of prices, which is the natural confequence, require.

From the confideration of our reftraints on importation of corn, whofe operations act as a bounty, you proceed to the confideration of the direct BOUNTY which our fyftem gives *on the exportation of corn,* to which you make the like, but ftronger objections. As you feem on this fubject to have adopted the reafoning which * Mr. Necker ufes, and to have copied it clofely; and as his book, as well as your's, will carry great authority with it, I will in this place examine both your objections *enfemble.*

Contrary to the common ufe made of the popular argument in favour of the meafure, you both fay, the meafure has a direct tendency *in the inftant* to raife the price of corn in the interior market, and to enable the merchant to introduce it into the foreign market at a lower price. What you fay is fact, and the truth rightly underftood; and yet while this meafure encourages a plenty, overflowing with a conftant fucceffion of furpluffes, it hath a tendency, *in a feries of times taken together,* to lower the price. That our meafure of the bounty has not been the fole caufe of lowering the price of corn, Mr. Necker gives a decifive proof in fact, which you † copy. That the general lowering of the price of corn is not owing to the Englifh meafure of *the bounty on exportation,* is (he fays) plain, becaufe the fame general lowering of the price has taken place in France in the fame period, where a direct contrary fyftem, *a total prohibition of exportation,* hath invariably prevailed till very lately. You add to his argument an affertion, " that it raifes however *not the real but nominal price only,* " and is of no ufe to the landed intereft." There is perhaps (you fay) but one

fet

* Sur la Legiflation & le Commerce des Graines.   † Vol. I. P. 248.

fet of men in the whole commonwealth to whom the bounty either was or could eafily be ferviceable, thefe are the corn-merchants; it loads (you add) the publick revenue with a very confiderable expence, but does not in any re-fpect encreafe the real value of the landed man's commodity.

Mr. Necker has alfo faid that the bounty is not neceffary; for if there be a furplus, and the foreign market wants it, it will have it without the aid of the bounty. The difference only is, that if the merchant finds that he cannot export it at the price of the Britifh market, fo as to carry it to the foreign market, he mut wait till it falls in price in England, or rifes in the foreign market, as many fhillings per quarter as the bounty would give: *then* he will be equally able to export it *without* as *before with* the bounty. In a corollary of which argument you join him in faying, as he had faid, that if the fur-plus quantity may be, by the aid of the bounty, thus exported when corn is at a high price, the furplus of a plentiful year will always fo go out, as not to come in aid to relieve the fcarcity of a defective one.

After having (in a manner indeed which rather has reference to the effect it might have in France) reprobrated the meafure of granting a bounty on the exportation of corn, he gives an opinion, in which I own I was furprized to find you following him; that if an encouragement is neceffary to agriculture, it fhould be given *not on the exportation, but on the production.*

I will firft ftate what I think to be the real operations and end of the boun-ty on corn exported, and then confider the pofitions above, not by way of re-ply, but by comparifon on fair examination, mark wherein they deviate and differ from the real ftate of the cafe.

Any country rifing in that progreffive ftate of improvement, by which Eng-land for near a century hath been rifing, muft have experienced *a continued in-flux of riches*; that continued influx muft have and hath created *a continued progreffive rife of prices.* If the continuation of the influx was arrefted in its courfe, however great *the quantity of* riches which hath come in, however great the glut of money; yet, after it hath fpread itfelf in all parts, and found its general level, *all* prices will be proportionably raifed; the original proportions which they held, before the ftart of prices, will be reftored; all therefore, how-ever high, will be but *nominal,* and a greater or a lefs quantity of the precious metals will be totally indifferent; but the cafe is very different, while the in-flux is in continuance. During its operation it ftarts the prices of things, but of different things with very different velocity in the motion of the rife. Objects of fancy, caprice, luxurious ufe, and the leffer articles of food, which bore little or no price, while the neceffaries muft always have born a certain price, even what may be called a high price in a poor and unimproved ftate of the commu-nity, will, when the progreffion of improvement begins, ftart firft in price, and with a velocity that will continue to *forerun* the velocity of rife in the price of neceffaries.

neceffaries. The relative proportion of the fcale of prices being changed, the difference of the prices is real, and corn will be always laft and loweft in the fcale. Although the price of corn may and will rife, yet not rifing in proportion to other things, and the rents of land and the wages of labour depending on the price of corn, the price of every other thing muft not only rife before rent and wages can ftart in price, but muft continue *fo to forerun* in their rife, that the landed man and labourer muft be in a continued ftate of oppreffion and diftrefs: that they are fo in fact, the invariable and univerfal experience of all improving countries, actuating manufactures and trades, demonftrates. In the end all muft equally partake of the general profperity; corn muft rife in price; rents muft rife; wages muft be encreafed: but during the continuance of the influx there muft be a partial diftrefs, which, although relative, is not the lefs but the more aggravated from being relative, others being in the actual enjoyment of a profperity which the landed man can but look up to and hope for in the end. If the operation was fhort, and if the influx foon fpread itfelf into a level, it would not be of much moment in what order the fcale of prices arofe. In a country where the land-workers and owners are few, in proportion to thofe employed in trade and commerce, as in rich commercial countries of fmall extent, there this effect is foon produced; there the landed intereft cannot fuffer much from the difproportionate velocity of the rife of prices, however accelerated; but in a trading and commercial country, *of large extent,* the fpreading and level of the inflowing riches muft be an operation of fo long time, and the effect fo far removed from the firft caufe, that the land-worker and owner can never receive a proportionate relief, much lefs the benefit of an equable fcale of prices, *while that caufe is in operation.* If the influx be a continued encreafing operation, the fcale will always be afcending. In a country circumftanced as thus defcribed, if the legiflator is ever to intermeddle, or can ever do any good by meddling in thefe matters, his interference fhould be directed to relieve this opprefled order and clafs of the community. The Englifh meafure of the bounty does this, by aiding in its firft effect the relative, and therefore *real price* of the produce of the land *without obftructing the natural effects* of the advancing and improving ftate of the community. It relieves the relative diftrefs, which the acceleration of the inflowing of riches occafions to the land-worker; it helps to accelerate the rifing of the price of his commodity, and in fome meafure guards them from a greater diftrefs, which they would otherwife feel: as it is, the traders and merchants eat out the landed man: they do fuffer, but much lefs than they would do. In a country of this fort the velocity of the influx of riches (efpecially if *an artificial influx* by paper money is added to the real one) may have even too much acceleration, if care is not taken at the fame time to accelerate alfo the diftribution of thefe riches into every channel and duct. In fuch a country as England, but more efpecially in

France,

France, if commerce be encouraged by the force of any artificial spring, if a disproportionate and * *more than natural* influx of riches comes in upon it, how much soever (when this influx may in the end have taken its whole effect and spread itself into a level) the land and labourer must necessarily share in the general prosperity, yet if care is not taken to give acceleration to the motion of the landed interest, in some proportion to the motion of the advance of commerce, and the influx of riches, the landed interest must remain under a continued depression of circumstances. Under this relative depression the land-worker, while he is buying every thing he wants at an advanced price, requires some adventitious force or spring to aid the velocity of the rise of the price of his commodity which he hath to sell. The wisdom of our ancestors, men of business, acting not from selfish and ungenerous motives, not from any jealousy of commerce, but from feeling and experience, gave this very encouragement, and gave it, in the very way in which it could have the truest effect; in which it could do the least harm, and the most good. They encouraged the land-worker without checking the operations of commerce, or retarding the progress of improvement: and while in the direct instant they effected by the bounty a rise of price to the saleable commodity of the land-worker, and gave that encouragement, which was thus become necessary; yet they so gave the bounty, as that in the remote effect it would prevent the enhancing of the general price, because the bounty encouraged the raising not only a surplus, but a succession of surplusses. They converted these surplusses even of our food into an article of commerce, and encouraged, and made it the interest of the corn merchant to trade with it in every part of the world.

Thus acted the homely understanding of the country gentlemen *upon practice*; men of refined and great abilities, speculating in the closet, *decide upon theory*, that it would have answered the same ends better to have given the bounty *not on exportation, but on production*.

As the bounty on exportation goes only to the surplus exported, and as a bounty on production must have gone to the whole quantity raised, which measure do you, who made the objection, think would load the publick revenue most? But unless there was an assured constant vent by exportation of any surplus that should be raised, such a bounty as you and Mr. Necker recommend, would never encrease the quantity, or raise a surplus, (for say you, B. IV. C. V. P. 123) " unless the surplus can in all ordinary cases be exported, the " grower will be careful never to grow any more than what the bare con-

---

* Either by an undue creation of paper motion, or by the bringing in great quantities of money amassed by conquest or by rapine, as was the case in Rome, by the money brought from Asia; as was the case in Britain, by the money brought from Indostan.

sumption

" fumption of the home market requires, and that market will be very fel-
" dom overftocked, but will be generally underftocked." To what end, fay
I, fhould the farmer work; it would be only making to himfelf work, to
lofe profit, for the more he raifed, the lefs would be the price.

On the contrary, the bounty on the exportation, at the fame time that it
doth (as you and Mr. Necker juftly obferve) actually and directly raife the
price of the commodity, it raifes (I fay) *not the nominal* but the *real* price,
for it brings that price which was *relatively* too low, nearer to the level of the
general fcale of prices : At the fame time that it is (as you truly fay) ferviceable to the corn-merchant, it enables him, without lowering the price of corn
below the rate at which the farmer in the country can afford to produce it, to
throw it into the general circulation of the commerce of Europe at an average
rate which fuits that commerce. This tends to encreafe, and does encreafe the
quantity raifed, and yet preventing on one hand a difcouraging fall, or a difproportionate inhancement of price on the other, keeps that price equable ; and
by creating a fucceffion of furpluffes, obviates your fear, that the exportation
of the furplus of the plentiful year fhould prevent the ufe of a furplus, which
fhould relieve, and come in aid to the defects of a fcarce one ; for it doth
actually, by the fucceffion of furpluffes, which the high prices of the home
market will always firft command, provide againft fuch fcarcity, which point
the regulations in the permanent corn law, of the 13th of G. III. on this
head do ftill more effectually fecure.

Let us now try how your's and Mr. Necker's objections to the Englifh meafure of granting a bounty on corn exported bear againft thefe operations.

Let us try Mr. Necker's firft objection, viz. that it is a meafure unneceffary, becaufe, fays he, if there be a furplus which the foreign market wants, it will take
it off, as foon as the home price falls, or the foreign prices rife, as many fhillings
in the quarter of corn as the amount of the bounty comes to. We fhall find, that
if no furplus of wheat, for inftance, can go out and flow in the channels of the
European market, at a higher price than 32 fhillings per quarter, (the general
average price of wheat in Europe) there will be no fuch furplus ; the farmer, in
the prefent improved ftate of England, loaded at the fame time as it is with taxes,
cannot afford to raife wheat at that price : And if the Britifh merchant did
wait till the Englifh wheat did fink to that price, he might better never export it ; he would find, that the Dutch, Hambrough or Dantzic merchant
had got to market before him, and had foreftalled it. On the other hand
confidering that, at the very loweft eftimation, the farmer cannot raife wheat at a
lower average rate than 37 fhillings per quarter, the bounty adds the five fhillings,
per quarter, which is juft fufficient on one hand to enable the merchant to
give the farmer a living price, and on the other to carry it to the foreign market at the average rates of that market ; fo that if the encouragement of the
farmer, and of the fupply be proper, and if " the bufinefs of the corn-mer-

chant

" chant be in reality that trade, (as you fay) which, if properly protected and
" encouraged, would contribute the moft to the raifing of corn."* This
meafure of a bounty on export is every way not only beneficial, but neceffary : although you have faid, in one place, that it is ferviceable to the corn
merchant *only*, yet in this view you yourfelf find, that this trade of the corn
merchant " will fupport the trade of the farmer, in the fame manner as the
" wholefale dealer fupports that of the manufacturer."

The next objection in which you and Mr. Necker join, is, that the doing
any thing to raife the price of *corn* (as you exprefs it, of *fubfiftance*, as Mr.
Necker rather more logically) in the home-market, muft of courfe raife the
expence of our manufactures, and give advantage to the rival manufactures
of every part of Europe againft us. This objection takes rife from a total
mif-ftating of the cafe.

If corn was the firft article which ftarted in price, fo that all other commodities followed it, then indeed both your pofitions would be true; firft,
that fo far as refpects the home market, we fhould only raife the *nominal*
price, for all rifing proportionably, there would be no alteration in the *ra-
tios of the fcale:* this would therefore be of no ufe to the farmer on one hand,
but by raifing *all the articles of fubfiftance and fupply*, our manufactures muft
become too dear for the average rates of the general market. But the contrary is the fact. Corn is the laft of all the articles of the market which
ftarts in its price, and rifes always with the floweft motion. It is only in
confequence of all other commodities having arifen, that a rife in this becomes neceffary, and when it does begin to rife, it follows with fuch unequal motion, that fome encouragement becomes neceffary, as a fpring to aid
the velocity of its rife in proportion to other things. It is not the rife of
the price of corn, but the general improved ftate of the country, raifing the
rates of all things, and the burthen of taxes fucceffively accumulated, which
raifes the price of our manufactures. On the contrary, encouraging the
raifing of corn by a good price in the direct inftant, creates a plenty : a
plenty, with a fucceffion of furpluffes, keeps down the price, taken in a general feries of times ; and in fome meafure it tends alfo to lower the price of
manufactures, by the number of hands which plenty of fubfiftance, if I
may fo exprefs myfelf, always creates.

Seeing then nothing narrow, invidious, felfifh, or ungenerous in our fyftem of reftraints and bounties on our corn trade, confidering it as a neceffary, wife and beneficial fyftem, interwoven into the general œconomy of
our agriculture, manufactures and commerce : perfuaded that a certain fober
conviction of experience, arifing from practice, firft fuggefted the truth, I
cannot but hope, that the fame wifdom which gave the bounty, will operate with the country gentlemen, to doubt every fpeculation of clofet doctrine,

* B. IV. C. V. P. 126.

trine, and to oppofe, on every occafion, every the moft diftant attempt to lower, or to confine within narrower limits this bounty.

You have made feveral obfervations on, fome objections to, and give rather a hafty and fummary judgment on the general fyftem of our corn laws; I have made fome remarks on thefe parts alfo, but I fhall referve thefe to another place, where I fhall have occafion to examine all the regulations relative to the fupply of the community with bread-corn, and to the manner in which the furplus of that fupply is converted into an article of commerce.

I will now proceed to the confideration of your opinions and doctrines refpecting the *monopoly of the colony trade.*

You allow, * " this colony-trade to be very advantageous, though not by " means, yet in fpight, of the monopoly, and that the natural good effects " of it more than counterbalance to Great Britain the bad effects of the mo- " nopoly; fo that, monopoly and all together, that trade, even as it is car- " ried on at prefent, is not only advantageous, but greatly advantageous." Although you allow this, yet while you confider our colonies " rather as a caufe of weaknefs than of ftrength", " as a fource of expence not revenue"; while you fay, that † " the invidious and malignant project of excluding other nations from any fhare" in our colony-trade depreffes the induftry of all other countries, but chiefly that of the colonies, without in the leaft encreafing, but on the contrary diminifhing, that of the country in whofe favour it is eftablifhed; that, in order to obtain a relative advantage, that country not only gives up an abfolute one in this trade itfelf, but fubjects itfelf to both an abfolute and relative difadvantage in every other branch of trade wherein this monopoly does not operate. While you fay this, you conclude, ‡ " that " under the prefent fyftem of management, Great Britain derives nothing " but lofs from the dominion which fhe affumes over her colonies." In confequence of this doctrine, you are not only for breaking up the monopoly, but for a difmemberment of the empire, § by giving up the dominion over our colonies. This prompt and hafty conclufion is very unlike the author of " the Treatife on the wealth of nations," it favours more of the puzzled inexperience of an unpracticed furgeon, who is more ready with his amputation knife, than prepared in the fkill of healing medicines. If we lofe our colonies, we muft fubmit to our fate; but the idea of parting with them on the ground of fyftem, is much like the fyftem which an ironical proverb recommends, " of *dying to fave charges*". When fuperficial importants talk, write, or vend fuch their idle crudities, one is not furprized; unworthy of notice they are neglected: but when a man, who, like yourfelf, hath joined practical knowledge to the moft refined fpirit of fpeculation, can fuffer himfelf fo to be miflead, an examination of thofe fpeculations, or at leaft of their confequences, as they lead to practice, is due to him and to the world: I will therefore examine your objections to the monopoly, and

the

* B. IV. C. VII. P. 194. † Ibid. P. 196. ‡ Ibid. P. 224. § Ibid. P. 224.

the reasoning whereon you found them, by the actual operations and effects of this colony-trade, acted upon by this monopoly.

But first I cannot but observe, that a round assertion, " that our colonies " have never yet furnished any military force for the defence of the mother " country, and that they have been a cause rather of weakness than of " strength", is such as should have followed only from a deduction of facts: and I will beg leave to suggest to you some facts that induce me, and may perhaps you also, to be of a very different opinion. That very naval force, which by their armed vessels they are now so destructively exerting against our West-India trade and transports, they did very effectively in the two late wars, especially in the last, exert to the ruin of the West Indian commerce of France and Spain, and to the almost total obstruction of all communication of those countries with their respective colonies. If you have not heard of what they did then, judge of it by what they are able to do now, against the whole undiverted power of their mother country.

The mother country, with her own immediate force, must always meet the immediate force of its enemies, wherever exerted. If therefore France sent its European forces to America, Great Britain, with her European force, must meet them in that field. If the strength of our colonies, exerted against the colonial strength of France or Spain was effective; or if it was ready to serve where it could best serve, and where most wanted; if it was not only equal to its own defence, but did act against the enemy offensively also, with effect, it did bring forth " a military force for the defence of the mother country." The military force of the province of Massachusett's Bay not only defended the dominions of the mother country in that province, but for many years exerted itself in defending Accadia or Nova Scotia. In the war which ended by the peace of Aix la Chapelle, the military force of that province took Louisburg and Cape Breton, an acquisition which purchased for the mother country that peace. So far as my assertion may go in proof, I will venture to assert, that had France during the last war effectuated a landing in Great Britain, and had been able to maintain themselves there until an account of it should have arrived in New England, I should have been able to have brought over, or sent from the province, Massachusett's Bay (perhaps joined by Connecticut also) " a military force " for the defence of the mother country".

On the point of revenue, I will also beg leave to repeat, because I have now still stronger reason for it, an assertion which I made in parliament, that before we went to decided war, a revenue might have been had upon compact, on terms which would have established the constitutional sovereignty of this country, regulating at the same time the trade and naval powers of the colonies, if those terms might have gone, at the same time, to the securing the rights of those colonies as granted by the government of that mother

country,

country. As to the ways and means of coming at the *grounds of agreement*, and the nature of that revenue and compact, an explanation never will be withheld, if ever again events shall render them practical. The colonies did always raise a revenue in support of that establishment of internal government, which the mother country had set over them; I do not say that I approve the manner in which they applied it. As to their raising, while *under a state of minority*, farther taxes, *except port duties*, for the *external purposes of the empire at large*, I will give no opinion, but submit it to your judgment, who have thoroughly considered the different fructuation of surplus produce expended in revenue, or vested in circulating capital, for further improvements, which further extend the British market in America, to decide, which of the two were, in that state, most beneficial to the mother country. I reason here in the line in which you consider the subject, the line of political œconomy, not of administration of government.

Your objections to the monopoly endeavour to prove, that, in *the invidious and malignant project* (as you stile it) of excluding as much as possible all other nations from any share in the trade of our colonies, Great Britain sacrifices, in a great degree, an absolute advantage, to enjoy in a lesser degree a relative one: that if the trade had been free and open, the industry of the colonies would not only have been less cramped, but the source of all the advantages deriving to Europe, from the settlement of Europeans in America, would have been more abundant and more productive of advantage: and that, although Great Britain had sacrificed a relative advantage which she derived from the exclusive trade, she would yet have had a greater absolute advantage; as an explanatory proof you instance in the monopoly of the article of tobacco. The market opened for this article would, you think, *probably* have lowered the profits of a tobacco-plantation nearer to the level of a corn-farm; the price of the commodity would *probably* have been lowered, and an *equal quantity* of the commodities, either of England or of any other country, might have *purchased a greater quantity* of tobacco than it can at present. I will suppose with you, that by this new arrangement, and the consequential *new ratio in the scale* of prices betwixt Europe and America, that Great Britain as well as other countries would have derived a great absolute advantage: yet as these other countries would have derived the same advantage from our colonies, this fancied absolute advantage could be but merely *nominal*; for although England thus got more tobacco for a less quantity of British commodities, yet as other countries also got the same on the same terms directly from Maryland or Virginia, what Great Britain thus got would not only be less in value, but would run the risque of being a drug upon her hands. In giving up therefore the relative advantage which she enjoyed by her exclusive trade, *while she gained a nominal*, she would lose every *real* advantage. Besides, there is surely some management to be observed in the culture of an article of produce, whose con-

sumption

fumption hath arifen from whim and caprice into an habitual, but not a neceffary ufe : inftead of encouraging an unbounded produce of this, it were beft, *probably*, that it fhould be limited. I am fure it is an abfolute advantage to Great Britain, that Virginia and Maryland fhould find it moft to their advantage to cultivate tobacco, rice, indico, or any other exotick commodity, than that by bringing the profits of a tobacco-plantation nearer upon a level with thofe of a corn farm ; they fhould find their advantage in raifing corn to the rivalling us at the European markets in our home commodity, and to the depreffion of our agriculture. So far therefore as this argument goes, it demonftrates to me, at leaft, that by quitting the relative, *a real* advantage, we fhould not even gain a *nominal* advantage, but fhould run every rifque of lofing every advantage, both relative and abfolute, real and nominal, which is to be derived from this fource reftrained, and at the fame time of fetting up a rival culture againft our own agriculture. If you fee the matter in this light in which it appears to me, you will, I am fure, feel how dangerous it is to vend thefe novelties of fpeculation againft the fober convi&tion of experience.

Your argument goes on to ftate, that there are *very probable reafons for believing*, that although we do facrifice this abfolute advantage (which would, *it is fuppofed*, probably be drawn from a free and open trade) for a narrow mean relative advantage ; yet we do not poffefs even this relative advantage, without fubjecting ourfelves, at the fame time, both to an abfolute and to a relative difadvantage in almoft every other branch of trade of which we have not the monopoly.

It ftrikes me as material, and I am fure, therefore, you will excufe me making, in this place, one remark even *on the manner* of your argument, and how *you ftretch your reafoning nicely.* You in words advance upon the ground of *probable reafons for believing* only, you prove by probable fuppofitions only ; yet moft people who read your book, will think you mean to fet up an abfolute proof, and your conclufion is drawn as though you had.

You proceed to defcribe thefe abfolute and relative difadvantages.

The monopoly of the colony trade, wherein the Englifh merchant was enabled to fell dear and buy cheap, gave a rate of profit in that trade much above the level of profit in any other, and would therefore never fail of drawing capital from thofe other branches into this, as faft as it could employ fuch. This double effect of drawing capital from all other branches of trade, and of raifing the rates of profit higher in our internal trades than it would otherwife have been, arofe at the firft eftablifhment of the monopoly, and hath continued ever fince. Having thus ftated the effect, you proceed to prove them to be bad and difadvantageous.

By drawing, not through the natural effects of trade, but by the artificial operations of the monopoly, capital from other trades, and other branches of trade in Europe, which were greatly advantageous both in a commercial and

in

in a political view, this monopoly, it is *probable* (you fay) may not have occafioned *fo much an addition* to the trade of Great Britain, *as a total change in
its direction.*

First, as to the affertion, that capital has been drawn from certain trades and
certain branches of trade in Europe, and turned by the monopoly into the colony trade, which without this would not have been fo diverted; that (I anfwer) is a matter of fact, which muft not be eftablifhed by an argument, *à
priori*—but on an actual deduction of facts. As I did not find the latter in
your book, I looked into the only records which we have of the progreffive
ftate of our commerce, in a * feries of returns of the imports and exports of
Great Britain, as made to parliament. I cannot afcertain in our European
trade that fact which your theory fuppofes. The tides and currents of commerce, like that of the ocean over which it paffes, are conftantly fhifting their
force and courfe, but this comes not up to your fact. I find no deprivation,
but an encreafed ftate of our European trade; and at the fame time an im-
menfe multiplied encreafe of our colony trade, and of every branch of commerce connected with it. Suppofing, however, that this fact was true, that
there hath been a *total change* in the direction of our trade, by drawing capital
from feveral of the European trades, and by employing more of our general
capital in the colony trade than would naturally have gone to it, had all trade
been free and open: yet that fuppofition will never, againft fact, prove, that
this monopoly, thus employing more capital in, and deriving more profits
from the colony-trade, hath occafioned a privation of advantage to the trade of
Great Britain in general—Fact contradicts that pofition. Well, but as Great
Britain cannot have fufficient capital to actuate all, it muft occafion a privation in fome of the branches of its trade; for, although there may not be an
abfolute decreafe in certain branches, there is a relative one, as they have not
increafed in the proportion in which they would have done. This is again
argument, *à priori*, in matters of fact, wherein it cannot act as proof; however, for the fake of your argument we will even fuppofe it, and afk the quef-
tion, what then? To which, in my way of reafoning, I fhould anfwer, that
as in the divifion of labour no one man can actuate all the branches of it, fo
in the divifion of the commerce of the world, no nation nor no capital can
carry on all the branches of it in every channel in which it flows. That country then which, while it does lefs in thofe branches of trade wherein leaft is to
be gotten, but has the command in that which exceeds all others in profit,
doth furely draw the greateft poffible advantage from commerce. This part
then of your argument proves to me, affifted by the reafoning which you ufe
in other parts of your work, the very reverfe of the conclufion which you here
draw from it.

You

* A very ufeful collection, publifhed by Sir C. Whitworth, M. P.

You say in the next place, that this monopoly has contributed to raise and keep up the rates of profit in all the different branches of the British trade higher than they would naturally have been, or, which is the same thing, to prevent them from falling so low as they would otherwise have fallen; and that this forced height of profit hath subjected the country, where it takes effect, both to an absolute and to relative disadvantage in every branch of trade, in which it has not the monopoly. I could here answer in general by your own reasoning, as you use it in the case of the profits of grazing and corn land; as when the state of the community is such, that it occasions a greater call for, and consequently a greater profit on the one than the other; that other will soon be converted into the one which is in demand, and will give the greater profits, till both come to a level: so in commerce, under whatever regulations, either those which the natural wants or the political institutions of men establish, it is carried on, will always shift about, and endeavour to flow in those channels wherein most profit is to be had. That country then which is under those fortunate and powerful circumstances, and has the wisdom so to profit of those circumstances, as to be able to maintain a monopoly of the most profitable channels; and be able to maintain, at the same time, (notwithstanding the clog of its high rates of profits) a share of other branches of trade, even where it is undersold, has surely acquired *that ascendency in trade and commerce*, which is always better understood than explained. But I will not rest within these entrenchments, I will meet your argument in your open field.

You say *, that in consequence of these high rates of profit, under which our commodities and manufactures must be brought to market, we must in our foreign trade " both buy dearer and sell dearer, must both buy less and " sell less;" but I deny the consequence, " that we must profit less," † because, although those high rates may confine the extent, yet raising the profit of the dealing, we enjoy as much, and produce in trade as much, as if we did more business of less profits: all is kept equal and level as to the foreign trade, and our colony trade goes on, the mean while, in a still more rapid prosperity. Your conclusion therefore, " that it is in this manner that the capital of Great " Britain has partly been drawn, and partly driven from the greater part of the " different branches of trade, of which she has not the monopoly; from the " trade of Europe in particular, and from that of the countries which lie " round the Mediterranean sea," is neither deducible from your argument, *à priori*, nor will you find it justified by fact

Yet again that we, who think well of the monopoly, may not derive any support from thinking, that as the colony-trade is more advantageous to Great Britain than any other, so the capital being forced into that channel, is of more advantage to the country than if employed any other way. That we

may

* P. 201. Vol. II.   † P. 219. ibid.

may not avail ourſelves of this comfort, you proceed to ſhew it to be " a na-
" tural effect of this monopoly; that it turns our capital from a foreign trade
" of conſumption with a neighbouring into one with a more diſtant country;
" in many caſes from a *direct trade* of conſumption *into a round-about one*,
" and in ſome caſes from all foreign trade of conſumption into a carrying one."
And as in the analytick part of your work you have ſhewn, that the direct
trade of conſumption, eſpecially that with a neighbouring country, main-
tains the greateſt quantity of productive labour, by the direct and frequent returns of its capital; that a round about trade is always leſs advantageous, and
the carrying ſtill leaſt ſo of all; you draw your concluſion, that therefore the
operation of the monopoly, thus acting, turns our capital into channels where
it employs leſs productive labour than it would naturally have done, if the
trade was left to its free and natural operations. By your firſt poſition you
mean, that it hath turned the capital from the European trade to the North
American and Weſt Indian trade, from whence the returns are leſs frequent,
both on account of the greater diſtance, but more eſpecially on account of the
peculiar circumſtances of America. An improving country, always dealing
beyond their capital, muſt wait to pay their debts by their improvements, by
which means, although the merchant may repay himſelf by the profit he puts
upon his goods, and by other means, yet the capital of Great Britain is detained and withheld; and, thus detained, prevented from maintaining ſuch a quantity of productive labour as otherwiſe it would do. In anſwer to this ſtate of
the argument (which I hope I have ſtated fairly) I ſay, that that part of our
capital, which is ſome while withheld in America, and does not return directly, is not withheld unprofitably to Great Britain: like that portion of the
harveſt which is detained for feed, it is the matrix of a ſucceeding and en-
creaſed production; by operating to advance ſtill farther theſe improvements,
and conſequently the population of theſe countries, it is *creating and extending
a new market*, whoſe demands for our productive labour calls forth that labour
faſter and to more advantage, than the ſame capital directly returned and
veſted in Britiſh goods could do; as it encreaſes this market in a conſtant pro-
greſſion, it calls forth more *manufacturers*; gives a ſpring to *agriculture*; and
extends the *commerce* of Great Britain.

Well but, ſay you, " ſecondly, the monopoly of the colony-trade has, in
" many caſes, forced ſome part of the capital of Great Britain from a direct
" foreign trade of conſumption into a round-about one." Wherever it does ſo,
that is an error in the ſyſtem, it ſhould be corrected and amended, ſo far as is
conſiſtent (as I ſaid above) with the eſtabliſhment of the unity of empire in all
its orders and ſubordination of orders. I have in a former part of this letter,
and many years ago on other occaſions, pointed out ſome of theſe errors and
their remedy; but I muſt beg here to apply thoſe diſtinctions, which, in my
remarks on the analytick part of your work, I ſhewed to exiſt in nature and
fact, *between a circuitous and a round-about trade*; and to obſerve, that where
your

your objections are pointed againft the circuitous operations of our colony-trade, they do not act with effect; for thefe are always advantageous, and fhould be even more encouraged than they are. Such a feries of fuch circuitous operations as create and extend the market, accumulating by each operation a frefh profit, return home not only (by this accumulated capital) with the means of employing more manufacturers, but with having created * an encreafing demand for more and more manufactures. The encreafing market of our improving colonies, ftill more and more rapidly improved by the circuitous trade, muft, while we have the command of that market, multiply Britifh manufacturers: thefe manufacturers thus multiplied, † " conftitute (as " you ftate it truly) a new market for the produce of the land, the moft advantageous of all markets, the home market, for corn and cattle."

Another objection yet remains, that in many cafes the colony-trade becomes, by means of the regulations of the monopoly, merely a *carrying trade*. This carrying trade, which you defcribe as a defect, would be fo, if the carrying was the only part in which our capital was employed, and the hire of the carriage the only profit that we derive from it; but inftead of that, joined as it is with the circuitous trade, it becomes, in a political as well as a commercial view, a beneficial part of the operations which employs our own fhipping.

Having gone through your argument of objection, you clofe with fome corollary obfervations, as deriving from it. You think, that the unnatural fpring applied to the colony-trade, has deftroyed the natural ballance which would otherwife have taken place amongft all the different branches of Britifh induftry, and that the direction of it is thus thrown too much into one channel. The idea then of a blood veffel, artificially fwelled beyond its natural dimenfions, ftrikes your imagination, and you are brought under an apprehenfion of fome terrible diforder. As this diforder did not feize Great Britain in the cafe you fuppofed, ‡ you then fearch out five unforefeen and unthought-of events (to which I could add another very perfectly forefeen and thoroughly underftood) which fortunately occurred to prevent it. As I am no *malade imiginair* in politicks, and have no fears of thofe § " convulfions, apoplexy, or " death," which have been fo often predicted, I know not how to go ferioufly, againft fact, into reafoning upon them. That our trade has felt, on a great and fudden fhock, no fuch convulfions or apoplexy, but that its productive powers continue to be actuated, and its circulation to run *in fome*

* This is what, in *the adminiftration of the Britifh colonies*, Vol. I. C. VIII. I call creating and fecuring " an encreafing nation of appropriated cuftomers ;" which idea you, from that fuperiority that fpeaking *è cathedra* always infpires, treat with fovereign contempt ; " it is, you fay, a " project fit only for a nation of fhop-keepers, governed by fhop-keepers." This idea, however, upon the clofeft and ftricteft analyfis is the only one I can find precifely to define the relation which a commercial country bears to its colonies, and to exprefs that inftitution of policy, in our act of navigation, which you rather too lightly and too contemptuoufly call (p. 222.) " a truly " fhop-keeper propofal."

† Ibid. 215. + P. 211. § P. 210.

other

other channels, though our American artery is obſtructed, proves, that this was not our principal, much leſs our ſole great channel of commerce; ſome part, perhaps great part, of our circulation paſſed through it into other remoter veſſels, which is now perhaps full as properly with more profit to the Britiſh merchant, poured through more direct channels. In ſhort, the whole ſtate of our trade, as it ſtands in fact, and is found in effect, is to me a proof in point againſt your caſe in theory.

" * The effect of the monopoly (you ſay) has been not to encreaſe the *quan-* " *tity*, but to alter *the quality* of the manufactures of Great Britain, ſuited to " a market from which the returns are ſlow," inſtead of keeping on in an old trade, " from which the returns are frequent."

If we conſider the effect which the opening a *new market under a monopoly*, or in *a free trade*, hath on a commercial country, we ſhall find, if it be a market which calls for ſome new aſſortment of manufactures of *a quality different* from the ordinary and accuſtomed ſort, in which that commercial country dealt before this new demand was opened, that *a free and open market*, into which the operations of a competition comes, *is more likely to alter the quality of the manufactures*, than where any commercial country poſſeſſes that market under a monopoly. In the former caſe they muſt watch and ſuit every call, every faſhion, and even caprice of their free cuſtomers; in the latter caſe they will oblige *their appropriated cuſtomers*, to take off ſuch goods as they pleaſe to ſend them, altho' the ſorts do not in quality entirely ſuit that market; they will under this monopoly, carry this ſo far as to drive the country, which is ſubject to the monopoly, into ſmuggling, not only on account of the price, *but merely to get goods of a quality which ſuits them*. Your great knowledge in the practick, as well as theoretick knowledge of our commerce, will be able to ſupply proofs of this fact from many revolutions of our manufactures in different periods of our commerce. It is not therefore *the effect of a monopoly*, ſo much as it would be *the effect of a free and open trade, to alter the quality* of the manufactures of Great Britain. We will then next enquire, *how this monopoly operates as to the increaſe or not of the quantity*. In the firſt ſtep we are agreed, that *this increaſing market of appropriated cuſtomers* doth at this one entrance *encreaſe the quantity* of manufactures demanded. Let us next enquire, how " the ſurplus produce " of the colonies, which (you juſtly ſay †) is the *ſource of all that encreaſe of* " *enjoyments and induſtry*, which Europe derives from the diſcovery and colo- " nization of America," operates under a monopoly, or would operate under a free and open trade to encreaſe the quantity of Britiſh induſtry and manufactures. The articles of this produce are (it is needleſs to enquire how) become of accuſtomed demand in the markets of Europe, not only for its more pleaſurable enjoyment, but in the line of induſtry alſo. So far as Great Britain hath

* P. 216.   † P. 193.

hath the monopoly of thefe articles, fhe will become *a neceſſary trader* in thefe markets. She will not go to fuch markets with thefe articles only; fhe will make up a cargo with affortments of her manufactures alfo; the one will neceffarily introduce the others; and if the firft cannot be had without the latter it will introduce thofe others, where, from the difadvantages of a high fcale of prices, they would not otherwife have been introduced; fo that *our monopoly* of thefe American fources of enjoyments and induftry to the Europeans, *doth not only tend to encreaſe* the quantity of our induftry and manufactures *partially, but abſolutely*. As they are interwoven with our general commerce, they do actually tend to introduce and carry on our commerce in our manufactures, even under thofe difadvantages, which you have defcribed as the effects of the monopoly; this is one ground of that *afcendancy in commerce*, which I rather referred to, than defcribed as enjoyed by Great Britain.

As to the fact about the returns of capital, if you will compare notes between the merchant trading in Britifh manufactures to Germany, and the merchant trading with Britifh manufactures to America and the Weft Indies, you will find the returns of the latter upon the whole (if thefe goods go no farther than North America, or our Weft Indies) not flower than thofe from Germany. Credit has, even before the prefent war, been extended in Germany, and fhortened towards America: inquire after this fact in Norwich, London, and the other great manufacturing places, and you will find it fo.

That the productive labour of Great Britain is kept down by the monopoly; that this monopoly prevents its affording revenue fo much as it might; and that rent and wages are always lefs abundant than otherwife they would be, is a corollary of propofitions neither proved by reafoning nor eftablifhed by fact. That the monopoly, raifing the rates of mercantile profit, difcourages the improvement of land, is ftill more aberrant from the line of reafon, and more directly contrary to fact: the reafon you give is, that the fuperior profits made by trade will draw capital from improvements in land. It will fo in the firft inftance; but as this encreafing advanced intereft of trade " conftitutes a new " market for the produce of the land,' the rates of the price of the produce of the land will fo rife, and fo raife the profits made by improvements, that, although at firft, as I have fhewn above, it fuffers a relative depreffion, the application of capital to it will of courfe and neceffarily become a very advantageous employment of fuch: but the new and daily encreafing market of America, of which we have the monopoly, raifing the rates of profit in trade, draws after it the daily afcending rates of that land, which fupplies this market and the workmen in it; and is the very thing coincident with a general profperity, that hath given fuch a fpring to agriculture in this country.

When you fay in another wreath of this corollary, that the high rates of profit neceffarily keep up the high rate of intereft, which *è contra* muft lower the value of land. I anfwer, that the rate of intereft does not neceffarily depend

pend on the rates of profit made by money, but on the proportion of demand for the ufe of it to the quantity which, and the velocity with which,
the *influx* of riches, in confequence of an advancing mercantile profperity,
brings it into circulation. High profits themfelves will occafion money to
come in to the market which wants it; high profits, and an increafing demand, will open and give birth to a fecondary fource by paper circulation:
fo that the major of your fyllogifm is not founded in reafon; nor is the conclufion, that the natural encreafe of rent, and the rife in the value of land,
is retarded by the effects of the monopoly, fact. I do here diftinguifh the
effects of the monopoly from the effects of the trade itfelf: this, like all
other advantageous applications of capital, where great mercantile profits are
to be gotten, accelerates the rife of the profits of trade fafter than thofe of
land; but thofe of land are in the effect raifed alfo by it; and although in a
flower degree of velocity to that of the rife of mercantile profit, *yet not in
a retarded but accelerated velocity alfo.*

Upon the whole, I fully and perfectly agree with you, that any regu-
lation which gives a *confined courfe of direction*, and keeps in that line of
direction any operation, muft check and deftroy part of the *vis motrix;* with
which the body moving would fly off in a *direct courfe.* Juft as the central
force, which confines any body to circulate round that center in any given
orbit, doth check and diminifh part of the projectile force with which it
would have flown off from that orbit: So the monopoly, which requires the
colony-trade to obferve Great Britain as its center, doth certainly check and
diminifh part of that *commercial activity with which it is at all points in
exertion to fly off in a tangent.* Although I agree in this truth, yet being
taught to think, that all feparate communities, until fome commercial mil-
lenium fhall melt down all into one, muft ever feek to give fuch a fpecifick
direction to the operations of their own fpecifick powers, as fhall maintain
the feparate and *relative ftate* of exiftence in which each community is
placed; and knowing it to be an univerfal law of nature, that in any machine, part of the original *momentum* muft always find itfelf diminifhed in
proportion as it becomes neceffary to give a *fpecifick direction* to its operation:
So I confider the lofing or leffening part of the productive activity, which the
culture and commerce of the colonies might give *in a direct line, that is,
to the world at large,* but not to Great Britain efpecially, as analogous to that
law of nature; as the very effence of that combination of force, and confequential fpecifick direction, which confines it circulating in an orbit round
Great Britain as its center; and as the precife ftate of that theorem, which
no politician in the one cafe, any more than any true mechanick in the
other, would deny as untrue, or condemn as wrong.

I cannot therefore but remain, and do fancy, that every fober man of bufinefs will remain in the perfuafion and conviction, confirmed by experience,

that

that while the monopoly of our colony trade gives as such to Great Britain, in its *relative state* of exiftence in the world, a *relative advantage* in the commercial world ; Great Britain doth not lofe unneceffarily any abfolute advantage, nor doth fubject itfelf to either abfolute or relative difadvantage, in all other branches of commerce in which it hath not the monopoly : That it employs our capital, upon the ballance of the whole, to the greateft advantage, and confpires in the means, together with other branches of trade, of drawing forth our utmoft productive induftry : And that under the true fyftem of a monopoly, Great Britain might derive from the dominion which fhe had in her colonies (of which dominion they were, in their due fubordination, part) *force, revenue, and every commercial advantage.*

These are the matters in which I think your book has erred. I have examined them with a view to fuch difcuffion, as may occafion a review of them ; becaufe I do really think, that your book, if corrected on thefe points, planned and written as it is, might become an inftitute, containing the *principia* of thofe laws of motion, by which the fyftem of the human community is framed and doth act, AN INSTITUTE *of political œconomy,* fuch as I could heartily wifh, for the reafons given at the beginning of this letter, that fome underftanding Tutor in our Univerfities would take up, as a bafis of lectures on this fubject.

I fhould here have proceeded to the confideration of your plans of the fyftem, which you think Great Britain fhould adopt in her future conduct towards America ; but the prefent ftate of events fufpends all political difcuffion on that head. If future events fhall ever lay a rational, found and true ground of colonial government, the propofing of fuch may then be proper, and fhall not be withheld. At prefent *jacta eft alea,* the fate of this country is now at the hazard of events, which force, and not reafon, is to decide. I am afraid we are reafoning here about things which once were, and were moft dear, but are no more.

I cannot conclude this letter without faying, that as I have impreffed upon my mind the higheft opinion of your abilities, learning, and knowledge, and think well of your fair intentions, I hope I have never deviated from the refpect which is due to fuch. I have taken pains to comprehend fully, and have meant to ftate fairly, your reafoning ; and to propofe my own, as I ought, with diffidence. If any expreffion breaths the fpirit of controverfy, inftead of what I meant, fair difcuffion, I difavow it ; for although perfonally unknown to you, yet from what I learn of you by your works, I find myfelf in every fentiment of refpect and efteem,

SIR,

Your moft obedient,

And moft humble Servant,

RICHMOND,
Sept. 25, 1776.

T. POWNALL.

F I N I S.